The Human Community

Where We Have Been
Where We Are Now
Where We Are Going

by Roy Charles Henry

The Human Community: Where We Have Been, Where We Are Now and Where We Are Going

Henry, Roy Charles

Copyright © October 2016, by Roy Charles Henry. All rights reserved. Create Space, a DBA of On-Demand Publishing, LLC. Printed in the United States of America.

ISBN: 978-0985717544

BLOG: http://mysimplereality.com

Design and graphics by Kevin Bradshaw

The Simple Reality Project:
A Pragmatic and Proven Plan to Create a Sustainable Human Community

by Roy Charles Henry

The Simple Reality Trilogy - The Three Great Questions Concerning the Nature of Reality

Where Am I? Understanding the Importance
of the Human Narrative

Who Am I? Understanding the Importance
of Human Identity

Why Am I Here? Understanding the Importance
of Human Behavior

Other Books by Roy Charles Henry

BLOG: http://mysimplereality.com

Science & Philosophy: The Failure of Reason
in the Human Community

Simple Reality: The Key to Serenity and Survival

Art in Simple Reality: Consciously Creating
Truth and Beauty

The ABC's of Simple Reality: An Encyclopedia of the Profound
Concepts Underlying the Paradigm Shift

Table of Contents

Introduction i

**Chapter 1   The Human Community:
Where We Have Been** 1

    Introduction 3

    The Evolution of American Identity 9

    Beware! The Nerds Are Ascendant: Bill Gates Is On the Move 23

    The Illusion of Change 29

    Crossroads 35

    History, Time and Progress 41

    A Brave Stupidity 47

    Solomon the Schmuck 53

    Power in Persia 55

    Jerusalem Day: Triumph or Disaster 57

    Doomed by Darwin in P-B 59

    In Search of P-A 61

    The Writing Is On The Wall 65

    Lost On The Ocean Blue 71

    Ghosts 77

    The Mirrors of History 85

    History: A Story, Your Story, Our Story And The Story 91

    History: His-story And Her-story 97

**Chapter 2   The Human Community:
Where We Are Now** 109

    Introduction 111

    The Ostrich 113

    Crazy Metaphors? Maybe Not! 119

    He's Onto Something! 125

Bad Choices 129

The Decline And Fall Of Practically Everybody 133

Feeding Frenzy: The Return Of The Stocks 137

Discouraging Compassion 143

Euphoria Or Dysphoria: Virtual Delusion 147

Happiness Is Pursuit Of Security, Sensation And Power—Not! 151

War Weary? 161

We Can Do This 169

Response or Reaction: Marshmallows, One or Two 173

Choosing Compassion 177

For Love or Money 179

Religion or No Religion? That Is the Question. Whether Tis Nobler ... Blah, Blah Blah 183

Chapter 3   The Future of the Human Community 187

The Robotic False Self 189

What Future? 197

Chapter 4   Insights—Community and Simple Reality 203

Absurdity 205

Cooperation and Competition 207

The Great Irony 213

Integration and Disintegration 215

Values 219

Appendix - The Point of Power Practice 221

Notes 227

Introduction

Nothing in our experience causes us more pain and suffering than the realization that we are failing to create a sustainable global community. Where did we go wrong? Are we capable of changing direction and exactly how would we do that?

This book, the fifth in the Simple Reality Project, focuses on the history of the human community, on human behavior in the present global village community, and finally on how we might or might *not* want to express community in the future.

When we speak of a study of history in the context of Simple Reality it does not have the conventional meaning most of us are conditioned to expect. For example, our study of history in this book is for the purpose of revealing a mirage so that it will disappear as we come to understand it.

We can all come together and choose to create a radically more satisfying experience of life by admitting what is really happening or continue in our behaviors of denial and distraction. We can transcend the illusion of history with the beliefs, attitudes and values of Simple Reality. That would be real, tangible progress.

Are we going to choose to wake up or will we choose to perpetuate our current nightmare?

CHAPTER 1
THE HUMAN COMMUNITY:
Where We Have Been

Introduction

Only a fool would try to compress a hundred centuries into a hundred pages of hazardous conclusions. We proceed.
   Will and Ariel Durant

There is indeed much wishful thinking involved in the subject of history. We are enamored of our story because it bolsters the false-self identity, an identity we cling to in fear hoping it will protect us from an imagined catastrophe that simmers just below the surface of our unconscious behaviors. We need a story that relates our progress, a story that promises things will get better, a story to affirm that we are indeed "the creature that reasons."

Those who cannot remember the past are condemned to repeat it.
   George Santayana

What is history? We usually think of history as a chronological record of past events and an analysis of those events. We analyze past events in the hope that we can come to understand how and why they occurred perhaps with the hope (as Santayana hinted) that the unpleasant events can be avoided in the future.

"Whatever the evidence may be, the popular notion of evolution, especially when applied by writers like Herbert Spencer to human society or civilization, connotes progress—the gradual yet steady march toward perfection. Apart from this application of the idea of evolution to man's world, progress seems to be the central thesis in the modern philosophy of history."[1]

There are a few thorny problems, however, with this notion of learning from history. First, as noted in detail in another of my books, "Time is a concept that humans created ... Time is a P-B construct created specifically to measure the experience of P-B and to assist in navigating the false self-centered paradigm."² Secondly, in the context of Paradigm B (P-B)ᵃ human experience never changes. In a Groundhog Day-like nightmare, there is a conditioned sameness to false-self behavior that virtually guarantees we will repeat the same mistakes, driven by the same delusional identity. We are stuck in a never-changing time warp.

> *Very few things happen at the right time, and the rest do not happen at all. The conscientious historian will correct these defects.*
> Herodotus—the "father" of history
> (5ᵗʰ century B.C.E.)

Herodotus seemed to have felt that much of history was a fiction and would have been dismayed to learn that it is *all* fiction. It *is* true that history, or the illusion called history, is written by the victors or the survivors to bolster the myth of their "exceptionalism." We humans search the story of our past hoping to find evidence that we are capable of creating a sustainable future.

> *History says, don't hope*
> *On this side of the grave.*
> *But then, once in a lifetime*
> *The longed-for tidal wave*
> *Of justice can rise up,*
> *And hope and history rhyme.*
> Seamus Heaney (1939-2013) Irish poet

We need much more than hope. Many of us would like to think that human history is a story of human progress. As much as we would like to put our history in a positive light, we have learned in Simple Reality that in the context of P-B any notion that humans have made progress on this planet would be an illusion.

ᵃ More about Paradigm A (P-A) and Paradigm B (P-B) can be found in *Simple Reality* published books and on the blog http://mysimplereality.com

Few historians are awake enough to even catch a glimpse of what human history is revealing. Will and Ariel Durant demonstrated what such insights beneath the illusion of "academic history" would be. Were they alive and writing history today, for example, they might have explained the historical significance of the growing chasm in America between the 1% and the 99%. They knew this historical pattern to be as old as humankind and they described it many times in their histories of ancient and modern civilizations. They sensed that these historical events were intrinsic to the story, identity and behavior of humankind, that is to say, built-in to the P-B story itself.

"Man is wicked not because he is born so but because he is rendered so. The great and powerful crush with impunity the indigent and unhappy. These, at the risk of their lives, seek to retaliate the evil they have received; they attack either openly or secretly a country that to them is a stepmother, who gives all to some of her children, and deprives the others of everything."[3] If history is any indication, the 1% will get their comeuppance. It's only a matter of time.

Cause and effect (what goes around comes around) cannot be escaped. The fates (the three goddesses who govern human destiny in Greek and Roman myth) will have their voices heard. The arrogance of the 1% "shapers" of history is especially noxious. The fates will quickly disabuse them of their illusions of power or about being favored by the neutral and inexorable movement of the story of Creation. Sometimes the fates reveal their sense of humor as they play topsy-turvy with the best laid plans of mice and men.

Conquered Greece took captive her barbarous conqueror.
Horace

Impermanence is (as Buddha made abundantly clear) an overriding principle in not only the experience of humankind but also in the flow of history: birth and death, emergence and evolution, decline and fall. Speaking of decline and fall, the decline and fall of Rome began as all human self-destruction does with giving free reign to the false self's darkest expressions including projecting onto the *other*. In this case the *other* was neighboring Greece.

Will Durant (1885-1981) is our correspondent reporting on how invasion and conquest always works both ways. "The Greek conquest of Rome took the form of sending Greek religion and comedy to the Roman plebs; Greek morals, philosophy, and art to the upper classes. These Greek gifts conspired with wealth and empire in that sapping of Roman faith and character which was one part of Hellas' long revenge upon her conquerors."[4]

"In Christian theology Greek metaphysics overcame the gods of Italy. Greek culture triumphed in the rise of Constantinople as first the rival and then the successor of Rome; and when Constantinople fell, Greek literature, philosophy, and art reconquered Italy and Europe in the Renaissance. This is the central stream in the history of European civilization; all other currents are tributaries. 'It was no little brook that flowed from Greece into our city,' said Cicero, 'but a mighty river of culture and learning.' Henceforth the mental, artistic, and religious life of Rome was a part of the Hellenistic world."[5]

Voltaire (1694-1778), a philosopher capable of deep insights, knew his own weaknesses and therefore also those of his fellow creatures. "Man is almost everywhere a slave. It follows of necessity that he is base, selfish, dissimulating, without honor; in a word, that he has the vices of the state of which he is a member. Everywhere he is deceived, encouraged in ignorance, and prevented from using his reason; of course he must everywhere be stupid, irrational, and wicked; everywhere he sees vice and crime applauded and honored; he concludes that vice is good, and that virtue is only a useless sacrifice ... If governments were enlightened, and seriously occupied themselves with the instruction and welfare of the people, and if laws were equitable ... it would not be necessary to seek in another life for financial chimeras which always prove abortive against the infuriate passions and real wants of man."[6]

Horace Walpole (1717-1797), English statesman, understood, however imperfectly, the futility of attempting historical progress as long as the false self was in control. "'We are totally degenerated in every respect, which I suppose is the case of all failing states' ... All mankind seemed to Walpole a menagerie of 'pigmy, short lived ... comical animals.'"[7]

"All in all, *The Decline and Fall of the Roman Empire* may be ranked as the supreme book of the eighteenth century."[8] High praise for a mere historian but we must remember that historians stick together and the Durant's had reason to respect this brilliant and insightful scholar, trapped as they all were within the worldview of P-B.

Edward Gibbon (1737-1794), given what he saw was the dominance of the false self, nevertheless was able to intuit that optimism grounded in the history of humanity was unwarranted. "He saw no design in history; events are the outcome of unguided [unconscious] causes; they are the parallelogram of forces of different origin and compromise the result. In all this kaleidoscope of events human nature seems to remain unchanged. Cruelty, suffering, and injustice have always afflicted mankind, and always will, for they are written in the nature of man."[9]

As long as humanity identifies with the false self and behaves according to that identity, progress will remain an oxymoron. The following essays will examine from a Paradigm A (P-A) perspective the historical record of human failure and why progress will remain elusive without a paradigm shift.

A paradigm shift involves a conscious choice—impossible for an unconscious person. Being unaware of P-A, the narrative most of us believe to be "real" (P-B) will overwhelm our best efforts to address what we perceive as obstacles to improving the human condition. The person acting on his intuition or in response to a profound insight can escape the clutches of history. He can then throw this book in the trash and dance.

The Evolution of American Identity

We shall be as a city upon a hill, the eyes of all people are upon us.
                John Winthrop (1587-1649)

Americans, let's be clear from the outset, your false self may be salivating at the prospect of discovering you are special—so-called American exceptionalism. Forget it! It ain't gonna happen because there is no evidence for it and swallowing that bunk in the first place is like gulping down hemlock. Let's try something "novel" called the truth.

It might be interesting, since professional historians are mesmerized by the P-B story, to see what writers of fiction would reveal about the fantasy that many Americans believe to be objective truth. Since the majority of Americans profess to be Christians of one sort or another, how well are we doing with "love they neighbor as thyself" and "love God with all thy heart, soul and mind"?

Now, for those of you who are still reading, your courage will be well rewarded; you will find out who you are and more importantly, who you are *not*. In the prose and poetry of American writers we will trace the evolution of the American false self with the occasional fleeting glimpse of the True self. Notice the key role that the American narrative plays in determining our shifting identity and, of course, the influence of both in explaining the unique behavior of Americans which turns out to be not so exceptional after all or at least, not in the way many of us might like to imagine.

In the beginning, of course, our identity was that of British subjects with the craving of our false-self security center salivating at the thought of opportunity in the New World. John Winthrop, who would later become the first governor of the Massachusetts Bay Colony looked across the pond and saw opportunity. "Why then should we stand striving here for places of habitation ... and in the meantime suffer a whole Continent as fruitful and convenient for the use of men to lie waste without any improvement."[1] How nice! Our earliest ancestors had the intention of "improving" upon the creation of Mother Nature. Axe in hand, off they went to "lay waste" to the whole continent, far beyond anything John Winthrop could have imagined. If by American exceptionalism we mean exceptionally destructive, we have indeed proved to be exceptional.

Only the best people came from the old sod, at least according to William Stoughton (1631-1701) who would later become a judge in the Salem witchcraft trials. "God sifted a whole nation that He might send choice grain over into this wilderness."[2] Maybe this attitude was the beginning of the idea of exceptionalism. "Choice grain?" You be the judge.

As we might expect, our ancestors were not free of the illusion of the *other*[b] and the tragic results of that delusion. William Bradford (1590-1657) of Plymouth Plantation expressed the belief common among his shipmates on the *Mayflower*. "Being thus passed the vast ocean and a sea of troubles … they now had no friends to welcome them, nor inns to entertain or refresh their weather-beaten bodies, no houses or much less towns to repair to, to seek for succor. [The] savage barbarians were readier to fill their sides full of arrows than otherwise."[3] But as H. L. Mencken would later humorously observe, the colonists were not the put-upon "innocents."

> *When the Pilgrim Fathers landed, they fell upon their knees—and then upon the aborigines.*
> H. L. Mencken[4] (1880-1956)

Our colonial ancestors were *exceptional* in their "violent" treatment of both nature and the American aborigines. We must also remember that these early New England settlers were Calvinists with a rather dark, if not ghastly worldview.

---

[b] More about the *Other* can be found in *Simple Reality* published books and on the blog http://mysimplereality.com

Like most of his contemporaries, the poet Michael Wigglesworth (1631-1705) wrote a long theological poem, the title of which revealed what was often on his mind.

The following excerpt is from his *The Day of Doom: A Poetical Description of the Great and Last Judgment*.

> *Before his face the heav'ns give place,*
> *   and skies are rent asunder,*
> *With mighty voice, and hideous noise,*
> *   more terrible than thunder.*[5]

In writing about the popularity of *The Day of Doom* many years later (after Calvinism was passing from Yankee New England), James Russell Lowell (1819-1891) probably had a good laugh when he cynically observed that it "was the solace of every fireside, the flicker of pine-knots by which it was conned perhaps adding a livelier relish to its premonition of eternal combustion."[6] Yes, the identity of many early New England settlers was that of being a "sinner," that is to say, exceptionally wicked.

As we read a portion of a sermon by the Reverend Jonathan Edwards (1703-1758), the prophet of the "Great Awakening" (a religious movement that began in New England in 1734), we hear the narrative that gave those sitting in the pews their guilt-ridden sense of self. "The God that holds you over the pit of hell, much as one holds a spider, or some loathesome insect, over the fire, abhors you, and is dreadfully provoked; his wrath towards you burns like fire; he looks upon you as worthy of nothing else, but to be cast into the fire; he is of purer eyes than to bear to have you in his sight."[7] That would have been enough to ruin one's "day of rest."

Harvard professor Sacvan Bercovitch (1933-2014) traced the origin of America's identity of "exceptionalism" to Puritan political and religious rhetoric. In his 1978 book *The American Jeremiad* "he discerned an American version of the jeremiad, a harangue [see Edward's rhetorical style above] about society's declining morals named after the biblical prophet Jeremiah. In this version, however, after berating an audience for its failings, the speaker would end up extolling the country as the world's best hope for redemption."⁸ Before we had even become America, our exceptionalism had extended to being the "Messiah" for the rest of the world, at least in the worldview of some Puritans.

We don't want to neglect the experience of the women on the American frontier. They had more responsibility for the survival of the community than their cousins back home and some at least felt that should come with more freedom. Enter Abigail Adams (1744-1818), the wife of President John Adams who said adequate schooling should be extended to "every class and rank of people, down to the lowest and poorest."⁹ We can hear Abigail saying to John, "If we mean to have heroes, statesmen, and philosophers, we should have learned women."¹⁰ Indeed, and so we can add an appreciation for education to the identity of our colonial ancestors.

An appreciation for the natural beauty of the New World also was evident early on in our history. The landscape painter Thomas Cole (1801-1848) painting the Hudson valley in the 1820s and 1830s lamented "They are cutting down all the trees in the beautiful valley on which I have looked so often with a loving eye."¹¹ As today, our materialism was in conflict early on with our sense of the good, the true and the beautiful. Our True self would wrestle with our false self throughout our history.

Poet William Cullen Bryant (1794-1878) reminded Cole as he left for a tour of Europe to not forget the Hudson River valley they both cherished.

> *Gaze on them, till the tears shall dim thy sight,*
> *But keep that earlier, wilder image bright.*¹²

In Simple Reality we have used New York City as the symbol of greed (the security energy center of the false-self survival strategy).ᶜ In *The New Yorker* magazine in 1839, Horace

---

ᶜ More about the false self energy centers symbolized by New York City, Las Vegas and Washington D.C. can be found in *Simple Reality* published books and on the blog http://mysimplereality.com

Greeley (1811-1872) takes us back to when greed was in its early stages in what was to become the "Big Apple." But that's not all. "New York has become the metropolis, in our country, not only of commerce but of literature and the arts. Like Tyre of old, she has covered the sea with ships, and her merchants are princes ... No man well acquainted with the history of Literature and Art in our country during the last ten years, can refuse to acknowledge that New York has towered above her sister cities."[13]

Many of our early writers became mesmerized by the cant of the myth of American uniqueness. In 1868 John William De Forest (1826-1906) published an essay titled "The Great American Novel" in *The Nation*. He thought Harriet Beecher Stowe's *Uncle Tom's Cabin* embodied the best in American idealism and promise for the future. To him America was a "populace of eager and laborious people, which takes so many newspapers, builds so many railroads, does the most business on a given capital, wages the biggest war in proportion to its population, believes in the physically impossible and does some of it."[14] As our earliest writers found much to praise in America, others began to look more deeply and began to see a darker side.

Another center from which the false self draws energy is that of sensation (sometimes called the affection and esteem center) which held a particular allure for Edgar Allan Poe (1809-1849). "I love fame—I dote on it—I idolize it. I would drink to the very dregs the glorious intoxication."[15] The sensation energy center is where our addictions reside. The poet Poe who also perfected the short story was intimately acquainted with the folly of self-medication. At only 40 years old, Poe was found dead drunk lying in a gutter on a Baltimore street. He died a few days later, was buried in an unmarked grave and forgotten for 26 years. Walt Whitman was the only prominent American to attend the ceremony in 1849 when the tombstone was placed upon Poe's grave.

One never knows for sure who is a mystic and who is not but Walt Whitman's art and behavior qualify him above all others in the flow of our history. Two others, Henry David Thoreau and Ralph Waldo Emerson studied the Bhaghavad Gita and Hindu mysticism.

While living at Walden Pond outside Concord, Thoreau (1817-1862) was amused by Irish laborers who came into the area to cut blocks of ice from the ponds for shipment around the world, including India. "Thus it appears that the sweltering inhabitants ... of Bombay and Calcutta, drink at my well. In the morning I bathe my intellect in the stupendous and cosmogonal philosophy of the Bhagvat-Geta ... I lay down the book and go to my well for water, and lo! There I meet the servant of the Bramin ... come to draw water for his master ... The pure Walden water is mingled with the sacred water of the Ganges."[16]

Thoreau understood, as did Buddha, that craving of any kind would cause suffering. A man is rich, Thoreau observed, "only in proportion to the number of things he can afford to do without."[17] We can appreciate in our own time, enamored as we are with our high-tech society, Thoreau's prescient warning *vis-à-vis* "technological toys." "Our inventions are wont to be pretty toys which distract our attention from serious things ... We are in great haste to construct a magnetic telegraph from Maine to Texas; but Maine and Texas, it may be, have nothing important to communicate ... As if the main object were to talk fast and not to talk sensibly. The nation itself, with all its so-called internal improvements, which by the way, are all external and superficial, an unwieldy and overgrown establishment ... tripped up by its own traps."[18]

Emerson (1803-1882) started his career as a Unitarian minister only to abandon it when he realized that all religions were too constricting. "It is the best part of the man that revolts from official goodness ... Whoso would be a man, must be a nonconformist."[19] In 1838 he delivered an address at the Harvard Divinity School and surprised the audience when "he attacked all formal religion and championed intuitive spiritual experience."[20]

Unlike many WASPS (White Anglo-Saxon Protestants) Emerson welcomed immigrants realizing that diversity would give the nation a more resilient identity. "The energy of Irish, Germans, Swedes, Poles, and Cossacks, and all the European tribes—and of the Africans, and of the Polynesians—will construct a new race, a new religion, a new state, a new literature, which will be as vigorous as the new Europe which came out of the smelting pot of the Dark Ages."[21]

And now back to Whitman (1819-1892). "An American bard at last! One of the roughs, large, proud, affectionate, eating, drinking, and breeding, his costume manly and free, his face sunburnt and bearded, his posture strong and erect, his voice bringing hope and prophecy to the generous races of young and old … Right and left he flings his arms, drawing men and women with undeniable love to his close embrace, loving the clasp of their hands, the touch of their neck and breasts, and the sound of their voices. All seems to burn up under his fierce affection for persons."[22] Not faint praise from the critic because *he* was the critic. This poet had to see the American exceptionalism in *himself* because no one else was paying attention to his poetry.

"Qualified" critics like Longfellow, Lowell, Holmes, and Mark Twain found little or nothing to praise in his *Leaves of Grass*. The problem was, as Whitman suspected, in the lingering Calvinistic prudery that had yet to take its last breath. Thoreau found several pieces in *Leaves of Grass* "disagreeable, to say the least; simply sensual. He does not celebrate love at all. It is as if the beasts spoke."[23]

> *Throwing myself on the sand, confronting the waves,*
> *I, changer of pains and joys, uniter of here and hereafter.*[24]

Whitman walked the talk of compassion—the acid test of present moment awareness—response! Going to visit his younger brother in Washington who had been wounded in the Civil War he remained there for three years caring for wounded soldiers from both the North and South.

> *On, on I go (Open doors of time! Open hospital doors!),*
> *The crush'd head I dress (poor crazed hand tear not the*
> *bandage away),*
> *The neck of the cavalry-man with the bullet through and*
> *through I examine,*
> *Hard the breathing rattles, quite glazed already the eye,*
> *yet life struggles hard,*
> *(Come sweet death! Be persuaded O beautiful death!*
> *In mercy come quickly.)*[25]

"H. G. Wells called [Stephen] Crane 'beyond dispute, the best writer of our generation.' *The Red Badge of Courage,* Wells wrote, 'was a new thing, in a new school ... entirely original and novel. To a certain extent, of course; that was the new man as ... a typical young American, free at last, as no generation of American had been free before, of any regard of English criticism, comment or tradition, and applying to literary work the directness and vigor ... there is Whistler even more than there is Tolstoy in *The Red Badge of Courage.*'"[26] Here emerges, if Wells is correct, our next type of American exceptionalism, namely originality.

History is not strictly speaking *belles lettres* but historian Henry Adams (1838-1918) had insights relevant to our theme of American identity. "His well-grounded pessimism subtly illustrated the transition of America during his mature years from an age of confidence to an age of doubt, and that, ironically, at a time the nation was reaching new peaks of material prosperity and scientific achievement."[27]

Adams had misgivings about the dehumanizing aspects of the American expression of the harsher aspects of the Industrial Revolution as Thoreau had earlier about the new technology associated with the Industrial Revolution. "I am wholly a stranger in it. Neither I, nor anyone else, understands it. The turning of a nebula into a star may somewhat resemble the change. All I can see is that it is one of compression, concentration, and consequent development of terrific energy, represented not by souls, but by coal and iron and steam."[28]

The World Columbian Exposition of 1893 held in Chicago foreshadowed the future of the America about which Adams had misgivings. The fairground was called the White City and its buildings displayed what the industrial and scientific future would look like. Carl Sandburg (1878-1967) would later describe it as the "City of the Big Shoulders."

Hog Butcher for the World,
Tool Maker, Stacker of Wheat,
Player with Railroads and the Nation's
*   Freight Handler ...*
Laughing the stormy, husky, brawling
*   laughter of Youth ...*[29]

Sandburg was not afraid to look at the particularly harsh reality of P-B emerging in such American cities as the turn-of-the-century Chicago.

They tell me you are wicked and I believe them,
for I have seen your painted women under the gas
*   lamps luring the farm boys.*
And they tell me you are crooked and I answer:
Yes, it is true I have seen the gunmen kill and go
*   free to kill again.*
And they tell me you are brutal and my reply is:
On the faces of women and children I have seen the
*   marks of wanton hunger.*[30]

In 1888, Edward Bellamy's utopian novel, *Looking Backward, or 2000-1887* expressed his doubts about the direction in which laissez-faire capitalism was starting to take the nation. "Conceived as 'a mere literary fantasy, a fairy tale of social felicity,' the book is actually a sharply pointed and skillfully directed exposure of the inadequacies of the private-enterprise system, of the inefficiency and material waste to which that system leads, and, worse, of the attrition of human values that results from it."[31]

The idealist Bellamy (1850-1898) imagined a paradigm shift conceived on the model of earlier American utopian experiments. "The story concerns a young Bostonian who awakens in the year 2000 from a sleep of more than a century to find that his familiar world has been utterly transformed. He awakens to a futuristic Brook Farm, so to speak, organized on a national scale. Under a new system of democratic collectivism, private enterprise has been abolished; state capitalism has replaced the great business monopolies of earlier times; social injustice, crime, poverty, and warfare have been eradicated.

Everything has been accomplished by orderly, democratic process. Under such benign and rational socialism, public intelligence and ethics have been raised to almost incredible heights. Man has conquered the machine, and all share equally in the abundant economy they have together helped to create."[32]

One way in which Americans were *not* exceptional, is that they never seriously entertained profound paradigm shifts and indeed according to several authors and poets, seemed to be moving into a relatively darker narrative.

As Bellamy looked forward to utopia, Willa Cather (1873-1947) saw the ideals of the hardy, pioneer spirit being replaced by the greedy predators of corporate capitalism. In her novel *A Lost Lady* she wrote: "The Old West had been settled by dreamers, great-hearted adventurers who were impractical to the point of magnificence; a courteous brotherhood strong in attack but weak in defense, who would conquer but not hold. Now all the vast territory they had won was to be at the mercy of men like Ivy Peters who had never dared anything, never risked anything. They would drink up the mirage, dispel the morning freshness, root out the great brooding spirit of freedom, the generous, easy life of the great landholders. The space, the colour, the princely carelessness of the pioneer they would destroy and cut up into profitable bits, as the match factory splinters up the primeval forest."[33]

Jack London's (1876-1916) *The Call of the Wild* is the story of a dog taken to Alaska, who becomes wild and travels with a wolf pack. Much of London's fiction is about the underlying savagery of the false-self masked by surface appearances, attitudes, beliefs and values. "Man himself is little better than an animal. 'Civilization has spread a veneer over the soft shelled animal known as man,' he wrote. 'It is a very thin veneer ... Starve him, let him miss six meals, and see gape through the veneer the hungry maw of the animal beneath. Get behind him and the female of his kind upon whom his mating instinct is bent, and see his eyes blaze like an angry cat's, hear in his throat the scream of wild stallions, and watch his fist clench like an oran-outang's ... Touch his silly vanity, which he exults into high-sounding pride, call him a liar, and behold the red animal in him that makes a hand clutching that is quick like the tensing of a tiger's claw, or an eagle's talon, incarnate with desire to rip and destroy.'"[34]

Edith Wharton (1862-1937) was awarded the Pulitzer Prize for *The Age of Innocence* (1920). She had been born into the leisure class of the vanishing Knickerbocker society of New York. Like Jack London, she saw beneath the veneer of the socially acceptable false self of those people "who dreaded scandal more than disease, who placed decency above courage, and who considered that nothing was more ill-bred than scenes except the behavior of those who gave rise to them."[35]

Another writer who saw that all was not well with the identity that Americans were choosing to perpetuate was Theodore Dreiser (1871-1945). He published the aptly titled *An American Tragedy* in 1925. "Dreiser saw the ruthlessness and the amorality of the world as aspects of a fundamental natural law that inexorably dictated the lives of men and women. There was in nature, he wrote, 'no such thing as the right to do, or the right not to do. We suffer for our temperaments which we did not make, and for our weaknesses and lacks, which are not part of our willing or doing.'"[36]

What is now being articulated by American authors is the exceptionalism of unconsciousness, not, of course unique to Americans.

Some say Robert Frost (1874-1963) was the most beloved American poet of the 20th century. In his poem "Fire and Ice" he revealed his acquaintance with his own false self.

Some say the world will end in fire,
Some say in ice.
From what I've tasted of desire
I hold with those who favor fire.
But if it had to perish twice,
I think I know enough of hate
To say that for destruction ice
Is also great
And would suffice.[37]

Frost intuited that human suffering had its origin in resistance to life as it is but was perhaps too optimistic in assuming that his fellow Americans would embrace the gift of life they had been given. Following is a portion of his poem "The Gift Outright."

The land was ours before we were the land's.
She was our land more than a hundred years
Before we were her people. She was ours
In Massachusetts, in Virginia,
But we were England's, still colonials,
Possessing what we still were unpossessed by,
Possessed by what we now no more possessed.
Something we were withholding made us weak
Until we found out that it was ourselves
We were withholding from our land of living,
And forthwith found salvation in surrender.[38]

Frost later regressed in his own personal identity away from feeling at one with nature toward his delusional false self. "In his earlier poems he describes the sometimes uneasy but always meaningful relation of man to nature. Man has need of nature, but nature has no need of man. Later he came to view the indifference of nature more as a hostile force with which man must struggle as heroically as he can. He regarded man in his earthly predicament with a detachment that ruled out any degree of compassion."[39]

Americans proved exceptional in failing to trust their own intuition, their inner wisdom.

John Dos Passos (1896-1970), in his trilogy of related novels, *U.S.A.* (1938), chronicled the American experience through most of the Depression years. "It is a tract of the times more than it is a timeless testament. It is a very sad epic that concludes in a massive indictment of American society. In his panoramic view Dos Passos saw American life only in terms of futility and frustration, corruption, and defeat for the individual, beyond hope of redemption by the most radical measures."[40] In his fiction, Dos Passos weaves incisive biographies of key Americans. One is labor leader Eugene Debs (1855-1926) advocating self-reliance, bringing us full circle back to Emerson.

"I am not a labor leader. I don't want you to follow me or anyone else. If you are looking for a Moses to lead you out of the capitalist wilderness you will stay right where you are. I would not lead you into this promised land if I could, because if I lead you in, someone else would lead you out."[41]

The Waste Land (1922), T. S. Eliot's (1888-1965) most famous poem, describes the postwar world as a desolate, sterile and chaotic place, one of the most striking depictions of P-B. The "waste land" is described as "an 'immense panorama of futility and anarchy' whose inhabitants are spiritually barren and desperate. Life is devoid of value."[42]

In his post-World War II essay "The White Negro," Norman Mailer (1923-2007) portrays an American identity traumatized by the horrors of concentration camps and the threat of the atomic bomb. "No wonder then that these have been the years of conformity and depression. A stench of fear has come out of every pore of American life, and we suffer from a collective failure of nerve. The only courage, with rare exceptions, that we have been witness to, has been the isolated courage of isolated people."[43]

Multidisciplinary artist Claudia Rankine (born 1963) manages in her work to look without blinking at the reality of the human condition, especially in America, her suffering homeland. The following is from her latest book (2014) *Citizen*. "The world is wrong. You can't put the past behind you. It's buried in you; it's burned into your flesh, into its own cupboard. Not everything remembered is useful but it all comes from the world to be stored in you ... Did I hear what I think I heard? Did that just come out of my mouth, his mouth, your mouth?"[44]

Well yes, Freudian slips can betray the bigotry and the fear of the false self. The *other* forever haunts our delusional identity. Rankine, who is African American, shines the light of truth on the darkest and seemingly never-ending chapter of American history. Why does this cancer seem so difficult to remove from our infected community? Simple Reality explains not only the resilience of this behavior but the treatment that would cure the patient.

In the mean time we must use every means at our disposal in our search for Truth, and our great writers make their contribution to that quest. The courage to write the truth after having the insights that reveal that truth is not common even in our best novelists and poets. For example, J. D. Salinger's (1919-2010) *Catcher in the Rye* "is at heart a *naïvely* passionate indictment of American phoniness and fallenness."[45]

In his 1950 Nobel Prize acceptance speech, William Faulkner (1897-1962) expressed his fear of the nuclear age and that bellicose aspect of the false self. And yet, he transcended that illusion and acknowledged the indestructible True self. "There are no longer problems of the spirit. There is only the question: When will I be blown up? I believe that man will not merely endure: He will prevail. He is immortal, not because he alone among creatures has an inexhaustible voice, but because he has a soul, a spirit capable of compassion and sacrifice and endurance."[46]

There you have it at long last—our true identity. There is nothing exceptional about it, it is universal.

Beware! The Nerds Are Ascendant: Bill Gates Is On the Move

Nerds can't help themselves because problem solving (in P-B) is their version of reaching the summit, of being "king of the hill." Nothing wrong with that; let them have their fun, right? Not exactly. In a previous volume in the Simple Reality series, *Science and Philosophy: The Failure of Reason in the Human Community*,[1] the title clearly communicates that we need to listen to the wise people, today and in the past, who have given a clear warning about being enamored of the human intellect.

The title of an article in *The New York Times Magazine* wherein Bill Gates and his friend David Christian extol the virtues of the intellect in "Everything Is Illuminated." That title should be followed by the simple word—*Not*!

Bill Gates (who admits being a nerd) likes to watch DVD's from the Teaching Company's "Great Courses" while he uses his treadmill. "On some mornings, he would learn about geology or meteorology; on others, it would be oceanography or U.S. history."[2] He discovered *Big History*, a Genesis-like synthesis or history of human knowledge created by the Australian professor, David Christian.

Christian's course divides history into eight "thresholds" beginning 13 billion years ago with the big bang which he calls Threshold 1. The origin of Homo sapiens is Threshold 6, the appearance of agriculture is Threshold 7, up to the modern world which is Threshold 8.

Christian's synthesis, an expression of the Homo sapien intellect, is an approach similar to how Simple Reality synthesizes the accumulation of human wisdom or the insights of human intuition, although Simple Reality is independent of history, space or time. Christian presents the "big-picture" of human knowledge in the context of linear time. Simple Reality transcends time and makes the distinction between what is "real" and what is an "illusion." Christian and Gates are trapped in the world of form in the structure of human consciousness composed of the illusion of the context (physical world), human identity (false self) and the resultant self-destructive human behavior (history). Nevertheless, "Gates started down the path to bring *Big History* to schools across the country."[3]

We all have two "guidance systems," so to speak, our intellect (also labeled the head) and our intuition (also labeled the heart, often called our inner wisdom). The intellect, as we are learning, is the guidance system in P-B; and our intuition is the guidance system in P-A (Simple Reality). Insights or intuition could be defined as original and deep or penetrating thoughts.

The foundation of the Hindu religion is found in the *Upanishads* which Schopenhauer praised for their "deep, original, and sublime thoughts."[4] (See the articles in Chapter 4 of this book for insights regarding the intellectual limitations of the "creature that reasons.")

The limitations of the human intellect were also understood by Shankara. "The world of thought and matter has a phenomenal or relative existence, and is superimposed [projected] upon Brahman, the unique, absolute reality. As long as we remain in ignorance (i.e., as long as we have not achieved transcendental consciousness [Simple Reality]) we shall continue to experience this apparent world which is the effect of superimposition. When transcendental consciousness is achieved, superimposition ceases."[5]

"There is nothing stranger in the history of religion than the sight of Buddha founding a worldwide religion, and yet refusing to be drawn into any discussion about eternity, immortality, or God. The infinite is a myth, he says, a fiction of philosophers who have not the modesty to confess that an atom can never understand the cosmos. He smiles at the debate over the finity or infinity of the universe, quite as if he foresaw the futile astromythology of physicists and mathematicians who debate the same question today."[6]

In the 16th century Christian worldview the intellect was sometimes thought of as synonymous with the personified devil.

"And finally all the worst deceptions which are caused by the devil, and the evils that he brings to the soul, enter by way of knowledge and reflections of the memory [conditioned reactions] ... For the devil has no power over the soul unless it be through the operations of its faculties, principally by means of knowledge."[7] Here St. John of the Cross, because of his extensive meditation in solitude, expresses his experience that the intellect can be used by the false self [the "devil" in his words] to distract us from Simple Reality.

> *We can understand wisdom in three ways: first, by meditation; this is the most noble way. Secondly, by being influenced by someone or following someone; this is the easiest way. Third is the way of experience; this is the most difficult way.*
> Tolstoy (1828-1910)[8]

Wisdom cannot be found by means of the intellect because it is not conventional knowledge. The Greek word *gnosis* often translated as self-knowledge, as in the Delphi oracles "Know thyself," is as Elaine Pagels says "better translated 'insight,' or 'wisdom.'"[9] She goes on to quote the Gnostic teacher, Hippolytus: "Abandon the search for God, and creation, and similar things of that kind [in other words, the world of form]. Instead, take yourself as the starting place. Ask who it is within you who makes everything his own saying, 'my mind,' 'my heart,' 'my God.' Learn the sources of love, joy, hate, and desire ... If you carefully examine all these things, you will find [God] in yourself."[10]

John Locke's (1632-1704) purpose in "*An Essay Concerning Human Understanding* was to inquire into the origin and extent of human knowledge, and his answer—that all knowledge is derived from sense experience—became the principle tenet of the new empiricism which has dominated Western philosophy ever since. Even George Berkeley (1695-1753), who rejected Locke's distinction between sense qualities independent of the mind and sense qualities dependent on the mind, proposed an idealistic philosophy in response to Locke's provocative philosophy and gave it an empirical cast which reflected Western man's rejection of innate or transcendental knowledge."[11]

What is this innate or transcendental knowledge? We know it well, those of us who rely on it as the gateway to an "experience of" rather than the "meaning of" life. A contemporary of Voltaire, Jacques-Henri Bernardin de Saint-Pierre put what we *and* he called "feeling" above reason. "The further reason advances, the more it brings us evidence of our nothingness; and far from calming our sorrows by its researches, it often increases them by its light ... But feeling ... gives us a sublime impulsion, and in subjugating our reason it becomes the noblest and most gratifying instinct in human life."[12]

Today we are involved in an historical struggle, a classic tug of war. It is the same struggle that occurred in France before the Revolution over 200 years ago "between Voltaire defending reason with wit and Rousseau pleading with tears for the rights of feeling."[13] Collectively, humanity has made its decision siding with Voltaire and the Enlightenment philosophers. It is, as we will come to regret, not the best one.

David Christian's approach to history is certainly intellectual and his *Big History: The Big Bang, Life on Earth, and the Rise of Humanity* includes 48 lectures on the facts the human senses have cataloged about the human experience. No, there is no "innate or transcendental knowledge," no hint of intuitive insights or the worldview of Oneness in these 48 half-hour lectures.

David Christian's course "financed by Bill Gates, [may] continue to grow as a regular history offering in high schools. The curriculum, which subsumes the role of humans within the larger context of geology, biology and astronomy, is not only fascinating but also offers students a worldview that places them as actors in this long sweep of Earth's history."[14] What's wrong with the *Big History* approach to teaching high school students about the world they live in? Most fundamentally, it's because P-B is not the Truth about the world they live in, and the identity they assume as "actors in this long sweep of Earth's history" is not a profound understanding of who they are or where they are.

By putting our eggs in the basket being carried by the human intellect, by following the nerds, we are being led astray. The nerds are once again on the move fleshing out the definition of P-B, and for those of us expecting a sumptuous breakfast of ham and eggs will instead find precious little to eat on our planet in the not-so-distant future.

There is only one truly "Great Course." It is called Simple Reality and it has the answers to any and all questions that are relevant to a suffering humanity.

The nerds may be on the move, but do they know where they are going?

The Illusion of Change

One purpose of the Simple Reality project is to foment change. To do that, we have to get your attention. How about a bit of tongue-in-check self-promotion to begin this essay: "Seventy-seven year-old sage Roy Charles Henry bursts onto the stage with a message of stark realism concerning the human condition. No one can afford to miss his latest book because no one will fail to experience the catastrophe described in it." Like that!

Or we can come up with relevant metaphors that capture the human imagination and help create energy for self-transformation. "The old ship Titanic is sinking, so abandon ship. Patching the gaping hole is not possible, so a radical change is necessary. We have to let go of our attachments to the old tub (P-B) and get in the lifeboats and row into the unknown." Like that!

But the damage is exaggerated, some will say. It can be fixed and repairs are already underway. O.K. let's go below and see if what those who are attached to the tried-and-true way of doing things are correct. Is the old ship (the old story P-B) still seaworthy and do we have the skill and wisdom, and enough courage and willpower to keep it afloat?

The latest research in human behavior suggests that *where* we are shapes *who* we are. In the language of Simple Reality, we say that our story determines our identity. Secondly, we have been making the case that the old ship is not a safe environment, it is toxic. Maybe the following will persuade those who are resistant to change to entertain a change in vessels.

An unhealthy environment shapes self-destructive human behavior and a healthy environment brings out the best in people. The false self in P-B is a fragile identity in that it doesn't exhibit predictable ethical behavior but is easily influenced by its context.

Most of us would like to think that we are consistent in our day-to-day expression of generosity and respect toward others and regard for our communities: "But the growing evidence suggests that, on some level, who we are—litterbug or good citizen, for example—changes from moment to moment, depending on where we happen to be."[1] This is the *relative* reality of P-B. (More about *relative* vs. *Absolute* later.)

"Most people, in fact, think of themselves as generous. In self-assessment studies, people generally see themselves as kind, friendly and honest, too. We imagine that these traits are a set of enduring attributes that sum up who we really are. But in truth, we're more like chameleons who instinctively and unintentionally change how we behave based on our surroundings."[2]

The "broken windows theory" is a relevant study that supports the influence of a P-B environment. "The theory's authors, James Q. Wilson and George L. Kelling, hypothesized in a 1982 article for *The Atlantic Monthly* that if the broken windows in a building were not repaired, people were more likely to break additional windows in the structure. And that, in turn, would only encourage more vandalism."[3]

In a related study experimenters littered a hospital parking lot and then put paper fliers on the windows of cars in the lot. Half the drivers threw the fliers on the ground as they left the lot. The next time the fliers were placed on the windshields of the cars but the parking lot was spotless. This time only 1 in ten drivers threw the fliers on the ground.

Hundreds of such studies over a period of several decades have supported the broken windows theory. "These studies tell us something profound, and perhaps a bit disturbing, about what makes us who we are: there isn't a single version of 'you' or 'me.' Though we're all anchored to our own distinct personalities, contextual clues sometimes drag us so far from those anchors that it's difficult to know who we really are—or at least what we're likely to do in a given circumstance."[4]

Because she is manned by sailors with vague and shifting identities it has not been smooth sailing thus far for the all of us trying to keep the global Titanic afloat.

We are adrift on the crippled and sinking ship of P-B without the anchor of our True-self identity; and to make matters worse, we are at the mercy of our reactive self and under the influence of our old-story self which will be blown hither and yon by the winds of the ethics of the ever-changing relative environment. We are not going to trouble ourselves with our behavior even if our ship is sinking if we think no one is looking at our behavior or is behaving the same way we are. This has been the self-destructive story of the voyage of the global Titanic from the beginning of human history.

Despite what sounds like a downer in assessing human history in the first essays in this chapter, we dare not forget the Truth concerning the voyage of humanity. All bad news is *relative*, i.e. it has no basis in Reality. Listen once again to our friend Einstein, more mystic than physicist. He intimated that the "Universe is friendly" meaning that Creation (One Mind) is perfect or there would not *be* any Creation. He was, of course, right about that and we can take comfort in the fact that *we* also must be perfect since Creation is one interrelated, interdependent and interwoven tapestry.

The rub is, we cannot enjoy that perfect Creation until we are conscious of the choices available to us. When we speak in this book of P-B, then, we are not referring to an actual alternative paradigm, but rather a "default story," a story resulting in our failure to awaken from our "fall" into unconsciousness. Even though the illusion of P-B doesn't in fact exist, for most of us it "appears" to be "out there." Therefore, when we speak of a study of history in the context of Simple Reality it does not have the conventional meaning most of us are conditioned to expect. Our study of history in this chapter is for the purpose of revealing a mirage so that it will disappear as we come to understand it.

What about the positive episodes in that epic historical voyage? Let us choose a modern twentieth century example that many of us remember or at least an historic event most of us are aware of. For example, India can be proud of the abolition of the caste system some 60 years ago. Right? Don't underestimate the influence of P-B upon Indian behavior or its history.

The castes were originally supposedly professional divisions but were eventually locked rigidly into place by birth and a structure of social rules that governed behavior both between and within them. Historically there were four main castes. At the top were the priests and teachers (Brahmins), next the warriors and rulers (Kshatriyas), third were the merchants (Vaishyas), and the laborers (Shudras). At the bottom the untouchables (Dalits), called Harijans or "children of God" by Mahatma Gandhi.

The Indian caste system today differs only in the details and is incompatible with a society that imagines itself as a democracy. For example, the Vaishya caste has the Gujarati Baniyas who specialize in finance, and the Brahmins have the Tamil who focus on math and classical music. "It's the equivalent in America of expecting the Asian kid to have good grades, the black man to be the best dancer and the Jewish guy to be well-read and have some slight mother issues."[5]

The caste system is vividly felt in both marriage and politics. Surveys reveal that almost half the voting population considers caste the most important reason to vote for a given candidate. Affirmative action is being used to help make up for the lack of education among the Dalits. Upward movement among the untouchables in Indian society has been slow. The vast majority of high paying jobs are held by the top three castes.

The attitudes, beliefs and values of P-B poison all of the world's societies. Even as a nation's people strive to become more tolerant of other classes, races and religions, the dynamics of politics continue to have a divisive effect on democratization. Fear-driven competition for what is perceived to be a limited amount of material wealth and power continue to drive the dynamic of shadow projection.

"As India transforms, one might expect caste to dissolve and disappear, but that is not happening. Instead, caste is making its presence felt in ways similar to race in modern America: less important now in jobs and education, but vibrantly alive when it comes to two significant societal markers—marriage and politics."[6]

The human false self has been controlling history, the cumulative record of human behavior, since we evolved into mammals with a brain conscious enough to remember our past. Only we can change the direction of that history and we are unlikely to do that without a plan. Remember, we are the creature that reasons, but we first have to become conscious. Until then our history, like everything else about us, is not what we imagine it to be.

Crossroads

Events are *historical* if they happened in the past and *historic* if they were deemed important by those who write an account of the human story. An "historic" encounter that almost no one knows about (but should) occurred between two distinctly different worldviews about the time Buddha was said to have lived. Had humanity understood the *historic* implications of what two ancient philosophers advocated, we might have arrived at a place today more congenial for our survival. More about those two philosophers in a moment.

An archetype or prototype is an original model or type or paradigm after which other similar things are patterned. Broadly speaking, we are historically committed to a paradigm chosen by our ancestors before we were born. Paradoxically, our *personal* narrative is one which we can choose but few people are aware of this. Hence, the widespread dissatisfaction many people have felt with their story (their "history") and their identity within that story.

Even our choice of behavior from moment to moment is not often felt by many to be something that they are *really* in control of. Nevertheless, many of us today delude ourselves that we *are* in control of our lives and that we can still stand at the crossroads of history and make a good choice. We *could* if only we knew what the choices really are. O.K. enough of that! What are those choices we don't know about?

Going back in history some 2,500 years we find humanity in China standing at a crossroads and two archetypal human beings who represent the two fundamental narratives still available to us today. Why are they still available to us today? Because our history whether as individuals or collectives is created in the timeless present moment.

Some historians believed these two Chinese sages, *Lao-tzu* and *K'ung-fu-tze* (Confucius) did meet and hence, did know one another. If so, their encounter must have seen some sparks fly because they had contrasting views of which road humanity should take, and indeed on the fundamentals of human nature itself.

In fact, the debate that did or would have occurred still takes place today—we call that conflict of choices or crossroads P-A or P-B. *Lao-tzu* (604-531 B.C.) is not his name but a description meaning "The Old Master" and the book attributed to him, the *Tao-Te-Ching* translated as the "The Book of the Way and of Virtue," is the basic text of Taoist philosophy. Notice how the following description resembles the worldview of Simple Reality.

The *Tao* means literally "a road." "Basically, it is a way of thinking [a paradigm], or refusing to think; for in the view of the Taoists thought is a superficial affair, good only for argument, and more harmful than beneficial to life; the Way is to be found by rejecting the intellect and all its wares, and leading a modest life of retirement, rusticity and quiet contemplation of nature [simplicity, solitude and silence]. Knowledge is not virtue; on the contrary, rascals have increased since education spread. Knowledge is not wisdom, for nothing is so far from a sage as an 'intellectual.' The worst conceivable government would be by philosophers; they botch every natural process with theory [think the 'War on Drugs']; their ability to make speeches and multiply ideas is precisely the sign of their incapacity for action."[1]

As we watch wisdom fade from the science-worshipping global village, Taoism also quietly makes its exit in modern China. "It is characteristic of Chinese thought [or used to be] that it speaks not of saints but of sages, not so much of goodness as of wisdom; to the Chinese the ideal is not the pious devotee but the mature and quiet mind, the man who, though fit to hold high place in the world, retires to simplicity and silence. Silence is the beginning of wisdom. Even of the *Tao* and wisdom the wise man does not speak, for wisdom can be transmitted never by words, only by example and experience. 'He who knows (the Way) does not speak about it; he who speaks about it does not know it. He (who knows it) will keep his mouth shut and close the portals of his nostrils.'"[2] Wisdom does not come through the senses or the scientific method.

Confucius (551-479 B.C.) on the other hand was passionate about morality (precepts) applied to everyday life and government. He counseled perfection without realizing that a faulty worldview resulted in a false-self that made that expectation unrealistic. "Not men but laws should rule ... and laws must be enforced until becoming a second nature to a society, they are obeyed without force."[3]

Will Durant shows how difficult it is to know what the history of humankind actually is by giving two conflicting assessments of the influence of Confucianism. "With the help of this philosophy China developed a harmonious community life, a zealous administration for learning and wisdom, and a quiet and stable culture which made Chinese civilization strong enough to survive every invasion and to remold every invader in its own image."[4]

Or is this what happened to China under the influence of Confucianism? "The rules of propriety, destined to form character and social order, became a straitjacket forcing almost every vital action into a prescribed and unaltered mold. There was something prim and Puritan about Confucianism which checked too thoroughly the natural and vigorous impulses of mankind, its virtue was so complete as to bring sterility."[5] Even the best of historians will get lost in the contradictions and ambiguity of the illusion of P-B.

Simple Reality teaches that Confucius had the cart before the horse. Moral behavior is the *result* not the *cause* of the awakening of the True self. We are naturally compassionate but not while under the influence of our unconscious false-self survival strategy. In 1993 in the village of Guodian in central China, bamboo strips were found in a tomb. "The texts on the bamboo, composed more than three centuries before Christ, emphasize that following rules and fulfilling obligations are not enough to maintain social order."[6] As the *Tao-Te-Ching* made clear, "The worst kind of Virtue never stops striving for Virtue, and so never achieves Virtue."[7]

Another historical crossroads which led humanity into the modern era occurred with the advent of modern science and the

Enlightenment. "It was conceptually impossible before the year 1700, about, for anybody in the world to say when religion began and politics ended. Trying to take religion out of politics and warfare would have been like trying to take the gin out of a cocktail."[8] Karen Armstrong understands as well as anyone that much of humanity is still immobilized at the crossroads, drunk on the poisonous cocktail of religion and politics.

Transcending both religion and politics is possible by choosing response over reaction in the present moment (Simple Reality). Mihaly Csikszentmihalyi's book *Flow: The Psychology of Optimal Experience* explains how our inner wisdom can be brought to bear in everyday life. Csikszentmihalyi's version of Krishnamurti's "I don't mind what's happening" is described in his "autotelic self" which translates potential threats into enjoyable challenges, and therefore remains in the Now experiencing the "feeling" of inner harmony. He would have agreed with Krishnamurti because he felt that "one can enjoy life even when objective circumstances are brutish and nasty."[9]

Returning to Americans, because they often found themselves standing at the crossroads of history, what did that process of choosing an American narrative look like? Boston was where the choice would be *historic*. The Boston "Brahmins" would make the choice; the Transcendentalists, trying as they did to wake up and offer an alternative, couldn't quite pull it off. If there was a moment in time when the choice crystalized, it was in 1857.

The occasion was the founding of the *Atlantic Monthly* with James Russell Lowell as editor. The magazine became a national institution almost overnight and a symbol of America's worldview. "Throughout America—in small rural towns, western cities, and eastern centers—thousands of subscribers eagerly awaited each new issue and thrilled at the works of its illustrious contributors."[10]

The path chosen at the mid-nineteenth century crossroads was religious morality but at least the most severe iteration, Calvinism, was abandoned. Oliver Wendell Holmes referred to the symbolic collapse of the Calvinist deacon's carriage in his poem "One-Hoss Shay."

> *You see, of course, if you're not a dunce,*
> *How it went to pieces all at once,*
> *All at once, and nothing first,*
> *Just as bubbles do when they burst.*
> *End of the wonderful one-hoss shay,*
> *Logic is logic. That's all I say.*

At this crossroads a science-based system of logic began to replace Calvinist predestination but continued to lead further away from human intuition and Simple Reality.

Our short essay on "spiritual travel" and choosing directions brings us to our own 21st century crossroads. "For as long as humans have walked, they have walked to get closer to their gods. The Babylonians made pilgrimages, as did the Greeks, Israelites, Chinese and Mayans. The Arabic word for pilgrimage, haji, comes from the Hebrew word for celebration, hag. In Tibetan, the word for human being means 'goer.'"[11]

So, where do we seem to be going today? Are we following the intellect-guided Boston "Brahmins" in the tradition of Confucian precepts focusing on morality, or are we tending to listen to our inner wisdom in choosing the "Way"?

We may not have yet chosen the high road to the present moment, but maybe we are headed back to the intersection that can take us there. Karen Armstrong might be pleased to hear that like the reaction against Calvinism in the 19th century, Americans and indeed the global village is turning away from mainstream religions.

Today's spiritual travel, while not yet conscious, is at least headed in a healthier direction. "In the United States, surveys from Pew and others show that attendance is down, membership is down, even the number of people willing to define themselves as religious is down. A 2012 Gallup study of 39 countries (from Asia to Africa) found a 'notable decline across the globe' in self-described religiosity, down 9 percent in just seven years."[12]

The worst that can happen to a human being is to allow oneself to be swept along by the "lights" of reason.
        Jorge Bergoglio (Pope Francis)[13]

But then there are those who cling to the Ten Commandments with a Confucian stubbornness. Don't worry David Brooks, we are not taking you to the woodshed again because that didn't seem to work with you. Obviously, Calvinism was not completely eliminated during the Yankee enlightenment and we must give the moralists their platform, with our tongue in our cheek of course.

As Mr. Brooks points out, "Religion may begin with experience beyond reason, but faith relies on reason."[14] Sadly, no! What is described by David Brooks is the human condition in a delusional paradigm, with an identity resulting in behaviors that are (as we see around us everywhere today) self-destructive. What we hope our struggling media pundits, our pandering politicians and pulpit grasping priests come to realize is that it is an AUTHENTIC experience well beyond reason that will lead us back to the crossroads where we will realize we have nowhere to go.

We stand perpetually each moment of our lives at the crossroads of intuition and the intellect, the decision point symbolized by the Taoist/Confucian archetypes. We allow our false self to obscure the simplicity of that decision and to paralyze our heartfelt choice of response over reaction, compassion over fear. Heaven is indeed already here and Now.

History, Time and Progress

I would there were no age between ten and three-and-twenty, or that youth would sleep out the rest; for there is nothing in the between but getting wenches with child, wronging the ancientry [the aged], *stealing, fighting.*
   Shakespeare: *The Winter's Tale*

Shakespeare's Bohemian shepherd was perhaps understandably jaded since Europe in the late 16th century was a harsh context in which to find a satisfactory life. Would shepherds today or anyone else say that the last 400 years have brought progress for humanity? Sounds like a ridiculous question, but is it?

The relationship among history, time and progress is not what most people would assume. In the *Syntopicon* of *Great Books of the Western World* we find that "progress seems to be the central basis in the modern philosophy of history."[1] Progress throughout human history is indeed "central" to the human story in P-B but whether that is true or not depends, of course, on how progress is defined. Western philosophers have tended to define progress as the slow and steady movement toward perfection.

In the beginning was the Word, and the Word was with God, and the Word was God. All things were made by him; and without him was anything made that was made.
   The Gospel according to St. John, *Bible*, John 1:1, 3

Nowhere in the Bible or in any sacred literature or wisdom of the mystics is anything said about the *Homo Sapiens'* capacity for the "slow and steady movement toward" the creation of perfection, or perfection of any kind for that matter. Creation as we humans will one day come to know was instant and complete as the Bible clearly states for those who can "hear."

> *And the light [perfect Creation] shineth in darkness [P-B]; and the darkness [unconscious false self] comprehended it not.*
> The Gospel according to St. John, *Bible*, John 1:5

We live in a perfect natural state which is obscured by our being asleep or, as they would tend to say in the East, mesmerized by ignorance. Believing that we will over time evolve into a state of perfection expresses this blatant and arrogant ignorance and flies in the face of our experience throughout our history.

We post-modern humans tend to think that technology and evolution are moving the "creature that reasons" forward. We have, after all, landed a man on the moon and conquered the scourge of most of the "old" diseases like measles, whooping cough, smallpox, polio, the plague, etc. Surely we have evolved into a more civilized species. We've had relative "peace on earth" for the last 40 years, that is to say, no world-wide wars.

But there are other criteria for measuring progress that we could and should look at. Happiness is difficult to measure but the mental health of a population would have to be considered a factor in assessing the success of a human community.

Many would cite the United States as one of the most technologically sophisticated and historically evolved of the world's nations. And yet! "The number of Americans who receive Social Security Disability Insurance for mental disorders has doubled during the past 15 years."[2] There are now (2013) 11.5 million American adults with a debilitating mental illness, on whom the country spends about $150 billion annually for therapy, drugs, and hospitalizations.

The mentally ill in America would probably not say that their experience of life is the result of human progress. "All together, our cumulative mental-health issues—depression, schizophrenia and bipolar disorder, among others—are costing the U.S. economy about a half-trillion dollars. That's more than the government spent on all of Medicare during the last fiscal year."[3]

Rates of suicide would have some relationship to how happy a given population perceives itself to be. In the U.S. the age group 50 to 64, the so-called Boomers, do not appear to be experiencing progress. "The suicide rate in this age group rose 45 percent between 1999 and 2010, with even higher increases for men in their 50s (a 48 percent rise) and women 60 to 64 (a 60 percent rise)."[4]

Let's return to the record of human evolution over the last 2,500 years in the West which was largely responsible for modern technology. Thucydides (471-400 B.C.E.) the Greek historian felt that humankind could learn from its history. "Knowledge of the past [is] an aid to the interpretation of the future, which in the course of human things must resemble if it does not reflect it."[5] Today it would be hard to make the case that humanity has learned from history as it attempts to create a sustainable community on earth.

Instead, we would have to conclude that self-destructive and unconscious people have dominated the unfolding human story. Adam Smith and Thucydides recognized the powerful influence that the security energy center or human acquisitiveness had on human behavior. "Both Smith and Thucydides judge economic improvement in terms of increasing opulence, the growth of capital reserves, the expansion of commerce, and the enlarged power in war or peace which greater wealth bestows."[6]

One thing that we can say we have learned from history, which Smith and Thucydides apparently didn't know, is that the accumulation of power and wealth is not progress. Aristotle (382-322 B.C.E.) was somewhat more insightful because he knew that the pursuit of plenty and power would not result in progress over time for humanity. "The avarice of mankind is insatiable; at one time two *obols* was pay enough; but now, when this sum has become customary, men always want more and more without end; for it is of the nature of desire not to be satisfied, and most men live only for the gratification of it. The beginning of reform is not so much to equalize property as to train the nobler sorts of natures not to desire more."[7] Aristotle like Buddha understood that one source of human suffering was craving.

Aristotle thought the improvement in human political institutions was the answer. Progress would be achieved by replacing the tribal form of government by constitutional government. He thought when kings and subjects were replaced by statesmen and citizens, progress would be realized.

Karl Marx (1818-1883) did not see capitalism as the path to progress. To him it was an improvement over feudalism on the way to communism. Progress to Marx was a classless economy. The bourgeoisie would overthrow the landed aristocracy and would create the proletariat which would in turn eliminate all obstacles to the perfect communist democracy.

Marx's theory of progress was that by improving institutions over time, humanity would also improve. This raises the question which, if we have been paying attention to history, we should be able to answer quite easily. Is progress accomplished by the improvement of human institutions or by improvements in the identity and behavior of humans?

Immanuel Kant (1724-1804) was able to imagine the "world state" (an inclusive United Nations) as the ultimate in political institutions. John Stuart Mill (1806-1873) had faith that democracy given enough time would "promote the virtue and intelligence of the people themselves."[8] Like Mill, Thomas Aquinas (1225-1274) thought progress was only a matter of time. "It seems natural to human reason to advance gradually from imperfect to the perfect."[9] Alas, time may be running out before humanity's ship reaches port.

For those who are paying attention, history teaches that neither human reason, nor the pursuit of wealth and power, nor the perfecting of human institutions results in progress for humanity.

In questioning human progress, we are not talking about the distinction between *absolute* and *relative* progress but instead whether humanity has made any progress at all. Comparing the global village to a pirate ship, we could use that old joke: "The floggings will continue until morale improves." The likelihood for historical progress, as it is defined in P-B, is slim indeed.

The "floggings" we just referred to on humanity's historical voyage refer to the universal truth that "life is suffering;" hence, our definition of progress would be the end or at least the beginning of the end of suffering. Does the record of human history show a lessening of suffering over time? Most of us would answer in the affirmative. Surely quality of life has gotten better over time in many areas of the world. But is that the same as reduced human suffering? Now we must define suffering to move our discussion forward.

Obviously what we are saying is that morale (the human condition) has not improved on our ship because flogging (suffering) continues unabated despite the fact that most of us would deny it as we point to human history. So who is right, the defenders or deniers of progress?

Risking overloading this essay with metaphors, we will move from the high seas to the plantation. Progress could be likened to freedom. A slave on a cotton plantation might feel he has made relative progress by being sold to a less sadistic owner and experiencing fewer or less vicious floggings. Whether he would admit it or not that slave may experience less suffering in a *relative* sense but there has been no progress in his fundamental situation. He is still a slave. He remains shackled within an institution inimical to his natural state as an awakened human being.

If Harriet Tubman shows up some evening and invites him to "follow the drinking gourd" would he have the courage to choose freedom?

And you? When you, dear reader, have a flash of insight while reading a Simple Reality essay, do you have the courage to make the tough decision to unshackle yourself from the slavery of living on the plantation of P-B?

Being whipped everyday by our Simon Legree-like overseer (our false self) we can hardly say that our history shows any progress. We are either free or we are not. We do not achieve freedom over time by intellectual or institutional progress. Freedom strikes like lightening in a blinding flash. One moment we are cowering slaves and the next, if we so choose, we are soaring eagle-like above the clouds of space and time, beyond all attachments to form, beyond the reach of suffering.

When we use the Titanic as a metaphor for the ship occupied by humanity we have to realize the only rational course of action for survival is to abandon ship before it is too late. Only a shift from the sinking ship (P-B) to a radically different vessel (P-A) holds any hope to end human suffering.

Or maybe you would relate better to a slightly different metaphor—we are like slaves on a pirate ship. Surely you can see that we cannot sail on a ship where flogging is seen as the way to improve morale or make progress. Remaining on such a pirate ship, the population of the global village might as well be beating a dead horse to make forward progress.

Suffering is easily defined in the context of Simple Reality as reactive behavior. Anyone who is reacting is suffering, anyone who is resisting life as it is, anyone who is not living in the present moment and embracing life's perfection is suffering. The ability to respond to life has nothing to do with history (when, where or what is happening) but everything to do with the story, identity and the resultant behaviors of the responder.

We can all transcend the illusion of history with the beliefs, attitudes and values of Simple Reality (P-A). That would be real, tangible progress and can be accomplished by anyone with the courage to let go of the sinking ship and the flogging pirate master—in other words let go of the pathetic pursuit of plenty, pleasure and power in P-B.

A Brave Stupidity

From the perspective of P-A every aspect of the story of human achievement will have to be rewritten and reinterpreted. Nothing will mean what it meant in P-B. To even attempt such an undertaking we would do well to acknowledge the caveat of the great historian Will Durant. "A history of civilization shares the presumptuousness of every philosophical enterprise: it offers the ridiculous spectacle of a fragment expounding the whole. Like philosophy, such a venture has no rational excuse, and is at best a brave stupidity; but let us hope that, like philosophy, it will always lure some rash spirits into its fatal depths."[1] We trust these "depths" will not be fatal but rather very healing.

Voltaire said, "I want to know: what were the steps by which men passed from barbarian to civilization?" We want to know something even more important: what steps will be necessary for humanity to pass from unconscious self-destruction to a sustainable experience of Simple Reality? Examining how we got to where we are and how different choices could have been made will be instructive in that regard. Humanity has yet to fulfill its destiny and will have to find a way to survive in order to do that.

Obviously, humankind got off to a bad start enthralled by the false self-survival strategy in the context of P-B. Instead of a story with Oneness as the guiding principle in a friendly and supportive Universe, we chose to construct our reality in what appeared to be a dangerous and competitive environment. As Will Durant confirms (in the 1950s), only fear was strong enough to overcome our deeper, truer compassionate nature. "He combines with other men because isolation endangers him, and because there are many things that can be done better together than alone; in his heart he is a solitary individual, pitted heroically against the world. If the average man had had his way, there would probably never have been any state. Even today he resents it, classes death with taxes, and yearns for that government which governs least. If he asks for many laws it is only because he is sure that his neighbor needs them; privately he is an unphilosophical anarchist, and thinks laws in his own case superfluous."2 Sound like anyone you know?

The second institution besides government to become an impediment to the experience of Simple Reality was religion. "The priest as magician," says Durant, "had access, through trance, inspiration or esoteric prayer, to the will of the spirits or gods, and could change that will for human purposes."3 And priests being human with a false self found that the gods wanted them to have more material wealth and power. "Religion begins by offering magical aid to harassed and bewildered men; it culminates by giving to a people that unity of morals and belief which seems so favorable to statesmanship and art; it ends by fighting suicidally in the lost cause of the past."4 In the march of human history at this point we have two failed institutions of P-B (government and religion) defining the unsustainable future for humanity. We are not so concerned with time, ironically, in this account of history but with the unfolding of illusion in the human mind.

We should pause at this point in our overview of the human narrative to consider the distinction between transformational or revolutionary change and transcendent change. "In one sense all human history hinges upon two revolutions: the neolithic passage from hunting to agriculture, and the modern passage from agriculture to industry; no other revolutions have been quite as real or basic as these."5 We can forgive Will Durant his inability to know about transcendent change, that was not his area of expertise after all and as an historian he is serving our purpose admirably well. The shift from P-B to P-A is much more profound than a transformational change.

Historical revolutions are a product of the human intellect working in the world of the relative, the paradigm of form both physical and mental. Transcendent change involves leaving the world of space/time, entering the present moment and experiencing our inner wisdom which connects us to the ongoing unfolding of Creation, an experience of ultimate Simple Reality. And now back to the unfolding of human history in P-B.

Time is not completely irrelevant. We can use it to get a sense of the flow of human experience that is so necessary to many a good story. Let us check into the story of humankind somewhere around 3000 B.C.E. Here we have a good illustration of the illusion of the *other*. When humanity decided the universe was unfriendly, then competition with other human beings for power, security and status became a common human behavior pattern. "In the competition of these two primeval centers [Kish and Ur] we have the first form of that opposition between Semite and non-Semite which was to be one bloody theme of Near-Eastern history from the Semitic ascendancy of Kish and the conquest of the Semitic kings Sargon I and Hammurabi through the capture of Babylon by the 'Aryan' generals Cyrus and Alexander in the sixth and fourth centuries before Christ, and the conflicts of the Crusaders and Saracens for the Holy Sepulchre and the emoluments of trade, down to the efforts of the British Government to dominate and pacify the divided Semites of the Near East today."[6] (As noted earlier, Durant was writing this in the 1950s.)

More recently U.S. troops are often called "Crusaders" by Middle Eastern Muslims today and the ages-old conflict is updated by the conflict between Israelis and Palestinians. We have only to substitute "American Government" for "British Government" to update the changeless pattern of Near Eastern history.

The Near East was the cradle of Western Civilization and seems to have set the pattern as this description harshly suggests: "To a distant and yet discerning eye the Near East, in the days of Nebuchadnezzar, would have seemed like an ocean in which vast swarms of human beings move about in turmoil, forming and dissolving groups, enslaving and being enslaved, eating and being eaten, killing and getting killed endlessly."[7] That was life in P-B then and it is life in P-B today. It is not our fundamental nature to behave like that, we simply have not chosen the best narrative. The P-B narrative we believe in determines an identity that is an illusion, and that identity drives our self-destructive behavior.

Of course, all of so-called history is in the eye of the beholder. We project our story onto the narrative that we imagine happened using the stories that we have been told and the physical evidence that remains to glorify and romanticize that which we want to have happened for our own false-self sensation center purposes. Take the Egyptian pyramids for example. "It is the memory and imagination of the beholder that, swollen with history, make these monuments great; in themselves they are a little ridiculous—vainglorious tombs in which the dead sought eternal life. Perhaps pictures have too much ennobled them: photography can catch everything but dirt, and enhances man-made objects with noble vistas of land and sky. The sunset at Gizeh is greater than the pyramids."[8]

The ego-driven false self is oblivious to the ominous fact of impermanence. The Roman emperor/philosopher Marcus Aurelius despite his status and power did not let that illusion blind him to the deeper realities of life and history. "Short then is the time which every man lives, and small the nook of the earth where he lives; and short too the longest posthumous fame, and even this only constituted by a succession of poor human beings, who will very soon die, and who know not even themselves, much less him who died long ago."[9]

Returning to ancient Egypt, we can again ponder how some tribes, empires and nations have been driven to amass material wealth, power and control over others, and to seek the admiration of others when all of this effort does not result in even the simple joys of solitude and silence. "Ramses II, one of the most fascinating figures in history, beside whom Alexander is an immature trifle; alive for 99 years, emperor for 67, father of 150 children; here he is a statue, once 56 feet high, now 56 feet wide, his weight a 1000 tons; for him Bonaparte should have used his later salutation of Goethe: 'Voila un home!—behold a man!'"[10]

In order to understand the development of P-B we keep our focus on the manifestation of the false self and how it continued to express itself in human institutions. What happened to compassion and morality in ancient Egypt? "In the end the connection between morality and religion tended to be forgotten; the road to eternal bliss led not through a good life, but through magic, ritual, and generosity to the priests."[11]

Now to Judea and a brief look at the history of humanity as seen in the Old Testament and Ecclesiastes written by an unknown author between 250 and 168 B.C.E. The author was a realist in that he began to define aspects of P-B. He realized that humanity was not going to "be soothed by any legend of a Golden Past, or a Utopia to come: things have always been as they are now, and so they will always be ... there is nothing new under the sun. Progress, he thinks, is a delusion; civilizations have been forgotten, and will be again ... Vanity of vanities ... all is vanity."[12] The narrative of P-B was neither going to deliver happiness nor a meaningful life and this author could see that long ago.

The same author foreshadows the teaching of Nisargadatta who warned that liberation is not achieved by having, doing and knowing. "I have seen all the works that are done under the sun, and behold all is ... chasing after the wind ... he that increaseth knowledge increaseth sorrow."[13]

Solomon the Schmuck

The words Solomon and wisdom are often found in the same sentence. Alas, wisdom and P-B are mutually exclusive and as we shall see Solomon certainly lived in an age when humanity was unconscious, very unconscious. Like most of us today he was controlled by his false-self energy centers seeking security, sensation and power.

Solomon was among the richest kings of his time and he was determined to protect those riches. "He repaired the citadel around which the city [Jerusalem] had been built; he raised forts and stationed garrisons at strategic points of his realm to discourage invasion and revolt. He divided his kingdom, for administrative purposes, into twelve districts which deliberately crossed tribal boundaries; by this plan he hoped to lessen the clannish separatism of the tribes, and to weld them into one people. He failed, and Judea failed with him."[1] Solomon had as much success attaining security as we do today—none.

Perhaps his purported wisdom helped him find fulfillment in the sensations of pleasure. "Some of his wealth he used for his private pleasure. He indulged particularly his hobby for collecting concubines—though historians un-dramatically reduce his '700 wives and 300 concubines' to 60 and 80 … Finally he resolved to adorn the city with a new temple for Yahveh and a new palace for himself … So for seven years the Temple rose, to provide for four centuries a lordly home for Yahveh. Then for thirteen years more the artisans and people labored to build a much larger edifice, for Solomon and his harem. Merely one wing of it — 'the house of the forest of Lebanon' — was four times as large as the temple."[2] And not a peep out of Yahveh—you gotta love that kind of chutzpah from the wise-guy. So did Solomon who never felt secure find happiness in sensual pleasures? You and I know that pleasure is just another word for suffering. Oh well! Maybe he could manifest his wisdom in attaining power.

Solomon was not wise nor was he religious despite his ostentatious temple. "Having established his kingdom, Solomon settled down to enjoy it. As his reign proceeded he paid less and less attention to religion and frequented his harem rather more often than the temple."[3] Don't worry, he knows what he is doing, this is Solomon after all. "The Biblical chroniclers reproach him bitterly for his gallantry in building altars to the exotic deities of his foreign wives, and cannot forgive his philosophical—or perhaps political—impartiality to the gods."[4]

Ah! He may not have been wise but he was smart. He used his marriages to forge political alliances to consolidate his power. But remember one of the principles of Simple Reality—impermanence—that is to say, nothing lasts. "No remains of the Temple have been found."[5] Poor Solomon! No security, no happiness from pleasure, and no power.

But before we feel too superior, are we wise-guys today? Fuugetaboutit! We are all about as wise today as Solomon was then and are having about as much success as he had in experiencing the present moment wherein lies all happiness, joy, peace, freedom and compassion. Wisdom is not a rare commodity in P-B, it is virtually non-existent.

Power in Persia

Religion, of course, has always played a powerful role in history and most religions manage to reveal profound aspects of P-A which, unfortunately, only a few of its followers ever understand. One such religion was Zoroastrianism in ancient Persia founded by Zarathustra; the date is uncertain, anywhere from 1000 to 600 B.C.E. The principle in question is that of the "Implicate Order" or source of Creation commonly called God today. The god of Zoroastrianism was Ahura-Mazda or the "Good Mind." Ahura-Mazda was more like the Greek Logos as the ever-present agency of Creation. Unlike the Christian God who "created" and "went home," Ahura-Mazda remained available to human beings to continue their part in the act of creation which was ongoing.

Human beings in this religion had both power and responsibility unknown in today's modern religions—they were expected to be self-reliant and exercise free will. They were active agents of the creative process or, if you will, creators of their own story, their own reality. This should sound more than vaguely familiar!

"Human beings were not, to Zarathustra's thinking, mere pawns in this cosmic war [between good and evil or true self and false self, if you will]; they had free will, since Ahura-Mazda wished them to be personalities in their own right; they might freely choose whether they would follow the Light or the Lie." The "lie" remains the same today as it was then—the toxic and unsustainable story centered upon the false-self survival strategy—which of course has a metaphorical character. The Satan of Zoroastrianism was Ahriman who "was the Living Lie, and every liar was his servant ... The soul of man, like the universe, was represented as a battleground of beneficent and maleficent spirits; every man was a warrior, whether he liked it or not, in the army of either the Lord or the Devil; every act or omission advanced the cause of Ahur-Mazda or of Ahriman."[1]

This was a religion that supported the possibility of human transformation and transcendence more than most of the religions that followed it throughout history. "All in all it was a splendid religion, less warlike and bloody, less idolatrous and superstitious, than the other religions of its time, and it did not deserve to die so soon."[2] Zoroastrianism believed in the possibility of Simple Reality. "It gave to the common life a dignity and significance grander than any that could come from a worldview that looked upon man (in medieval phrase) as a helpless worm or (in modern times) as a mechanical automaton."[3]

The worst sin in Zoroastrianism was unbelief. Unbelief was the equivalent of surrendering to the darkness, to Ahriman, to the false self. Such is our sin today. To believe in our own authentic power, to become self-reliant and to rely on our inner wisdom and our connection to the infinite possibilities of our connection to the "Good Mind" would be our victory over the Lie, and the return of the Light.

Jerusalem Day: Triumph or Disaster

Obviously, history, like beauty, is in the eye of the beholder. What to one person might seem a triumph, to another appears to be a tragedy. Few objective observers, however, would find it difficult to see a positive outcome for the nation of modern Israel. For Israelis, the story and future of their nation is not so simple. And for the embattled city of Jerusalem, the direction being taken is even more uncertain.

Jodi Rudoren is able to capture the confusion and conflict among many Israelis concerning the future of Jerusalem in her review of Yossi Klein Halevi's book *Like Dreamers: The Story of the Israeli Paratroopers Who Reunited Jerusalem and Divided a Nation.*

Jerusalem Day celebrates the capture of East Jerusalem from Jordan in the 1967 war. Not everyone views this victory over five Arab armies in the six-day-war as a good thing, not even all Israelis. For example, a resident of Gush Etzion, a suburb of Jerusalem, considers the outcome of the six-day-war a miracle and wonders why others do not.

Another secular Israeli considers the East Jerusalem settlement of half a million Jews will make resolving the conflict with the Palestinians impossible.

The author of *Like Dreamers* describes his book as "a story about the fate of Israel's utopian dreams, the vast hopes imposed on this besieged, embattled strip of land crowded with traumatized Jewish refugees."[1]

Yisrael Harel an advocate of building more West Bank settlements takes Arik Achmon, an airline executive, on a tour of what he is building in the West Bank. Achmon was impressed but he saw a different outcome than did Harel. "You and I, Arik thought, represent opposite visions of Israel ... Here in this romantic landscape, thought Arik, was rising the greatest mistake in the history of Israel."[2]

The title of Halevi's book *Like Dreamers* is a reference from Psalm 26 about the Jews returning to Israel. But those who have returned and those Jews of Middle Eastern origin constitute a divided nation. Zionists who have ignored their own laws to build West Bank settlements are on one side of what they see as the unfolding history of Israel; and on the other side are those both within and outside Israel who see the settlements and even the East Jerusalem occupation as immoral obstacles to peace and progress.

The last chapter of the history of Israel has already been revealed by the principles found in Simple Reality; it will not be easy to watch.

Doomed by Darwin in P-B

Will Durant says that, "In the eyes of a Darwinian world success would sanction every means."[1] He means by this, we think, that most individuals and nations will do whatever it takes to survive. In P-B, a worldview of scarcity, with the *other* always threatening on the horizon, perpetual violence is assured in the global village. Notice how World War II in the Pacific theater was inevitable given the way the Japanese saw "reality."

"Out of such conditions [P-B worldview] imperialism is born—that is, the effort of an economic system [people seeking security, sensation and power] to exercise control, through its agent the government, over foreign regions upon which it is believed to depend for fuels, markets, materials or dividends. Where could Japan find those opportunities and those materials? She could not look to Indo-China, or India, or Australia, or the Philippines; for these had been preempted by Western powers, and their tariff walls favored their white masters against Japan.

"Clearly China had been placed at Nippon's door as a providentially designed market for Japanese goods; and Manchuria—rich in coal and iron, rich in the wheat that the islands could not profitably grow, rich in human resources for industry, taxation and war—Manchuria belonged by manifest destiny ['every means' and every rationalization] to Japan. By what right? By the same right whereby England had taken India and Australia, France Indo-China, Germany Shantung, Russia Port Arthur, and America the Philippines—the right of the need of the strong. In the long run no excuses would be necessary; all that was needed was power and an opportunity."[2]

Individuals and nations do not have either rights or power; these are all illusion. All that exists in the march of evolution of the human narrative is fear driving the lust for property (plenty), pleasure and power. Illusion, illusion, all is illusion in P-B. And until we change our narrative, it leads us to suffering, endless suffering.

In Search of P-A

Whereas Will Durant sees the expression of the materialism of the security energy center of the false self as characterizing American identity, it is wisdom that he sees as dominating the identity of the ancient Greeks. "Greece respected wisdom as India respected holiness, as Renaissance Italy respected artistic genius, as young America naturally respected economic enterprise. The heroes of Greece were not saints, or artists, or millionaires, but sages; and her most honored sages were not theorists but men who made their wisdom function actively in the world."[1] To the degree that the Greeks' highest aspiration was wisdom, to that degree Greeks sought to create P-A. To the degree that the highest American aspiration is material wealth, to that degree Americans seek and of course succeed in creating P-B.

Being the birthplace of Western civilization, understanding the Greek worldview and evolution of Greek culture gives humanity insights into the current human condition. "When we look for unifying elements in the civilization of these scattered cities we find essentially five: a common language, with local dialects; a common intellectual life, in which only major figures in literature, philosophy, and science are known far beyond their political frontiers; a common passion for athletics, finding outlet in municipal and interstate games; a love of beauty locally expressed in forms of art common to all the Greek communities; and a partly common religious ritual and belief."[2]

The unifying elements of a common culture were made possible by a critical turning point in the history of Western civilization which occurred in the year 479 B.C.E. "The Greco-Persian War was the most momentous conflict in European history, for it made Europe possible. It won for Western civilization the opportunity to develop its own economic life—unburdened with alien tribute or taxation—and its own political institutions, free from the dictation of Oriental kings. It won for Greece a clear road for the first great experiment in liberty; it preserved the Greek mind for three centuries from the enervating mysticism of the East, and secured for Greek enterprise full freedom of the sea."3

Of course, in the context of Simple Reality, this split of intellect from intuition, of purely rational thought from mysticism, committed Western civilization to an unsustainable narrative, a self-destructive outcome.

Nevertheless, the benefits to humankind flowing from the Greek experiment were many. The aspirations to democracy, however imperfect, began in the Athens of Pericles (463-431 B.C.E.). "'Everyone would admit,' says Isocrates, 'that our laws have been the source of very many and very great benefits to the life of humanity.' Here for the first time in history is a government of laws and not of men."4

The names of the great philosophers are unknown to the masses but the names of the spiritual masters are universally familiar. History has a partial answer as to why this is so. Will Durant says, "The Greeks offered the East philosophy, the East offered Greece religion; religion won because philosophy was a luxury for the few, religion was a consolation for the many."5 That explanation is as true today as it was then. The mass of humanity flees its own false-self, seeking in religion a distraction and finding delusion.

We meet our destiny on the road we take to avoid it.
   C. G. Jung

The Greek philosophers struggled to discover the nature of reality and although they did not succeed they moved humanity forward in its understanding of the relative world, the world of P-B. "Every Greek colony poured the elixir of Greek art and thought into the cultural blood of the hinterland—into Spain and Gaul, Etruria and Rome, Egypt and Palestine, Syria and Asia Minor, and along the shores of the Black Sea."6

Durant continues, "The views of Greek poets, mystics, philosophers and scientists were scattered through scholars and students into every city of the Mediterranean concourse."7

"The Byzantine Empire wedded Greek to Asiatic culture, and passed on some part of the Greek inheritance to the Near East and the Slavic north. The Syrian Christians took up the torch and handed it to the Arabs, who carried it through Africa to Spain. Byzantine, Moslem, and Jewish scholars conveyed or translated the Greek masterpieces to Italy, arousing first the philosophy of the Schoolmen and then the fever of the Renaissance. Since that second birth of the European mind the spirit of Greece has seeped so thoroughly into modern culture that "all civilized nations, in all that concerns the activity of the intellect, are colonies of Hellas' today."[8]

The Greeks did their best in the search for truth and beauty. Truth eluded them but the legacy of beauty left to humanity shines around the world today.[d]

---

[d] It can be said that Greek civilization ended in 325 A.D. with the founding of Constantinople and the beginning of the Christian Byzantine civilization.

The Writing Is On The Wall

The only thing we learn from history is that we don't learn from history.
          Hegel

After I began to make the choice to respond and stay present as best I could, everything about my life began to change, to shift. For example, probably because I had been a history teacher for three decades, I could see that the entire chronicle of human history would have to be re-written to make sense in the context of P-A. Not just the "what happened" but more importantly "why it happened." Simple Reality provides a perspective from which we can see deeply into why human behavior occurred as it did and how to redirect the course of the human meta-narrative as well as the experience of the individual.

When I began to write this essay three titles popped into my head.

- The Decline and Fall of Rome and the U.S.A.
- The Decline and Fall of Practically Everybody
- The More Things Change, the More They Stay the Same

This happens often with essays and I usually pick the title that best conveys the central message of the piece. However, in this case, all three titles communicated something that is important and I wanted to keep them all. I ended up with yet a fourth and different title that I liked even better, but the original three remain as a central part of the essay itself, as you shall see.

The history that humanity has experienced is the history that we have chosen, albeit for the most part, unconsciously. If we have been choosing unconsciously, is that really a choice? Good point!

Throughout our history a number of individuals have tried to direct our attention to the same thing that this essay is trying to do. How we choose to live our lives moment-to-moment determines our history over time. If we insist on not hearing the message of the mystics or our own inner wisdom, we are choosing. To not choose is to choose. To choose P-B is to not choose P-A. To flee from our own inner awareness is cowardly, it is surrendering to fear; it is the same as writing a history, chapter after chapter, of unchanging darkness.

The unfolding disaster taking place all around us is nothing new and we all know it is happening. We humans are highly resistant to making choices that appear to be difficult. "Go with the flow" we seem to say even though we know deep down that we are headed for chaos. Long term benefits are not attractive; we want relief now. "Just gimme the pill doc, I am not going to make a lifestyle change." "I don't want to acknowledge my suffering; I want a distraction, an escape, a plausible denial."

Given that human behavior, regardless of when in history it occurs, is driven by the same false self and the same fears, we can expect an amazing consistency in the evolution of human communities, empires and nations. People have usually chosen what seemed to them at the time the "quick fix," the "easy way out," the "illusion of pleasure," anything to avoid "thinking things through."

There have been no successful communities in the history of humanity given that P-B and a sustainable "gathering" of Homo sapiens is mutually exclusive. You will see what we mean when we compare the self-destructive behaviors of ancient Romans with modern Americans. Only the details are different.

In his history of the Roman Empire Will Durant reveals the presence of the false-self security center operating in both Rome and the U.S. "The older Romans used temples as their banks, as we use banks as our temples."[1] Great insight, don't you think? Will Durant is no run-of-the-mill historian. The more things change, the more they stay the same indeed—think Wall Street, politicians, lobbyists and corporations—think greed run amok.

Rome did not have to produce goods; it took the world's money (borrowing sovereign funds from other "nations" if you will as America does from China and Japan today) and used it to pay for the world's goods. Public works were expanded beyond precedent[e] and enriched "publicans who lived on state contracts; any Roman who had a little money bought shares in their corporations. Bankers proliferated and prospered; they paid interest on deposits, cashed checks, met bills for their clients ... made or managed investments, and fattened on such relentless usury that cutthroat and moneylender became one word."[2]

"Houses [in Rome] became larger as families became smaller; furniture grew lavish in a race for conspicuous consumption."[3] "Clodius, leader of the plebs, built a mansion costing 14,800,000 [cisterces] ... Other villas rose on the hills outside of Rome; rich men had several, moving from one to another as the season changed."[4] And in America today? "The average home price in this mountain town [Aspen] has increased over the past four years, to $6 million in 2010."[5] As in ancient Rome, many of these "villas" in Aspen are second homes.

No matter where we look in human history, the false self is consistent in its behavior, only the details of story and identity vary. The "pleasure" of wealth and power has always been a source of suffering for all of us whether we lived in an ancient Roman villa or a $30 million mansion overlooking Aspen Mountain.

In fact, maybe the more wealth and power the more suffering. "The Aspen area is suffering from what some here describe as an epidemic of emotional crises and suicides ... This is not a new problem for Aspen. The suicide rate here has loomed above Colorado's already–high average for at least a decade."[6] Colorado has the 10th highest suicide rate in the nation (2014).

---

[e] Public works in the U.S.: think Halliburton and the 400 Americans (the 1%) whose wealth now equals all the rest of their fellow Americans' "wealth" combined (the 99%). Moneylenders in the U.S.: think Goldman Sachs, *et. al.*

The rising obesity rates in the U.S. had their equivalent in Rome as citizens stressed by the bewildering and scary behavior of their fellow citizens turned to food for distraction and escape. In America we all recognize the health crisis associated with compulsive eating. "'The citizens,' Cato mourned, 'no longer listen to good advice, for the belly has no ears.'"[7] The sensation energy center of the false self encourages conspicuous consumption and not only in spacious Roman villas and Colorado "second homes." In Rome, "Good chefs fetched enormous prices on the slave auction block. Drinking increased; goblets had to be large and preferably gold."[8]

Taking into account the size of the American defense budget, we can see that the false-self power center and the magnitude of fear in America are closely related. It was no different in Rome. "All in all, its revenues were modest; and like other civilized states it used them chiefly for war."[9]

Rome had borrowed freely from the culture of the Greeks but abandoned the fields of amateur sport for the spectators' benches as the spirit of the Olympic Games and amateur sports faded. These ancestors of the ubiquitous American "couch potato" were getting their exercise vicariously, leaving fun and games to the professionals, at great cost to the body and the soul. "Men became brave by proxy; they crowded the amphitheater to see bloody games, and hiring gladiators to fight before them at their banquets ... When a band of flute players attempted a musical concert ... in 167 [A.D.], the audience forced the musicians to change their performance into a boxing match."[10] The musicians in questions were probably slaves and had no choice in the matter and neither did the doomed gladiators killing each other in the various arenas throughout the Roman Empire.

The modern day American gladiator usually doesn't face such an immediate death but increasing numbers of professional and amateur football players today are experiencing injuries that are leading to mental illness, dementia and all too often a slow and unglamorous death.

The security center of the false self had a dominant role in life in ancient Rome just as it has in contemporary American culture. "The old morality ... could not keep this new regime of mobile capital from setting the tone of Roman life. Everyone longed for money; everyone judged or was judged in terms of money. Contractors cheated on such a scale that many government properties—e.g., the Macedonian mines—had to be abandoned because the lessees exploited the workers and mulcted [milked] the state to a point where the enterprise brought in more tribulation than profit."[11]

How did all of this affect politics? We only have to observe the partisan warfare going on in Washington and our state capitals in the so-called "culture wars" (2011) to understand perfectly the manifestation of the false self in the expression of politics in ancient Rome. "The aristocracy [oligarchy, i.e. the wealthy and the ruling class] which ... had once esteemed honor above life adopted the new morality and shared in the new wealth; it thought no longer of the nation, but of class and individual privileges and perquisites; it accepted presents and liberal bribes for bestowing its favor upon men or states and found ready reasons for war with countries that had more wealth [think oil producing nations in modern times] than power ... Within this aristocracy there was an oligarchy of dominant families."[12]

Similarly, for example, in U.S. history we had the Astors (fur), the Harrimans and the Hills (railroads), the Mellons and the Morgans (bankers and financiers), the Carnegies and Fricks (steel), the Du Ponts (chemicals), the Fords (automobiles) and the Rockefellers (oil). This veritable rogues-gallery of "Robber Barons" had their toga-wearing counterparts in Rome and we continue to have their Gucci-wearing counterparts today.

Let's return to Rome and our perceptive friend Will Durant. "The causes and forces of discontent, however, were too deep and varied to be easily dissolved."[13] "There were plebeians who had forfeited their property through defaulted mortgages [and] insolvent debtors and ruined speculators who had lost all hope or wish to meet their obligations ... A few revolutionists were sincere idealists, convinced that only a complete overturn [like many Tea Party members today] could mitigate the corruption and inequity of the Roman state."[14]

Mistrust of politicians was justified then as today as the false-self pursuit of power made it easy to forget the legitimate business of the state. Both Rome and Washington epitomize human corruption in their respective times. "Cicero's brother Quintus drew up for him a manual of electioneering technique. 'Be lavish in your promises,' Quintus advised; 'men prefer a false promise to a flat refusal … Contrive to get some new scandal aired against your rivals for crime, corruption, or immorality.'"[15]

As in America today, there were renegade artists in ancient Rome plying the streets and alleyways in search of a prominent "canvas" on which to display their current inspiration or outrage. "The exterior [of stucco houses] was … often defaced with graffiti—'scratchings' of strictly fugitive verse or prose."[16] Indeed, when it comes to history, the writing is on the wall!

Lost On The Ocean Blue

Columbus sailed the ocean blue ...

To the intellect history is either an enigma or a story that *seems* to reveal the motives of human behavior over time. And yet after millennia of evidence our narrative remains inexplicable to most of us. We are missing something. So maybe we need to look again at our story—this time with a more discerning, or perhaps more penetrating gaze.

We begin with a brief analysis of the nature of the concept of this business called the *story*. Those who know about such things tell us that a story contains *conflict* or two opposing forces, one called a *protagonist* (one who struggles "for") and the *antagonist* (one who struggles "against").

Now we bring our "penetrating gaze" into play. The structure of consciousness revealed in Simple Reality enables us to identify the True self as the protagonist and the false self as the antagonist.

Next, narratives are either *accomplishment* or *decision* stories. The accomplishment story is one "in which the protagonist or main character tries against opposition to achieve some goal; the second is that story in which the protagonist is forced to choose between two things—two sets of values, say, or two courses of action."[1]

Ah ha! Can you feel the narrative not only thicken but begin to come into focus? The True self as protagonist is trying to wake up but the conditioning of the false self is a powerful force *against* that happening. The True self is also challenged—confronting choices—first, between two paradigms (P-B and P-A); secondly between two identities (determined by the outcome of the process of the first choice); and thirdly between two dominant behaviors, namely reaction or response (suffering or transformation) also driven by the identity chosen in the second step. Notice how our history is woven together in a web of cause and effect. We don't tend to understand our history, our day-to-day experience in this way. This has caused us enormous problems.

For example, many Americans learned that the history of America began with Columbus in 1492, not with indigenous peoples crossing the Bering Strait land bridge or with the Vikings, as both were relegated to the abyss of the *other*. The story we wanted to tell ourselves about American exceptionalism needed the Italian explorer because he was white, European and a Christian. He was also a false self on steroids.

Columbus in his negotiations with Ferdinand and Isabella of Spain revealed the universal cravings of the false self. We are all familiar with these basic human desires; only the details differ from person to person. Columbus agreed to sail west from Spain to Cipango (Japan) and then on to the Indies. He would be the vanguard of both the imperial ambitions of Spain and opportunities for the Church as well.

The energy that drives history is well known to the readers of Simple Reality.

False-self energy centers	The 3 G's used by teachers of history	Columbus' contract and/or goals
Security/Survival	Gold	Percentage of riches discovered
Sensation (affection/esteem)	God	Missionaries harvesting new souls
Power/control	Glory	Title: Admiral of the Ocean Seas

And finally we find *irony* operating in the history of humanity. Put simply, we find contrast throughout the unfolding of our story between what *is* and what *ought* to be. Is our experience inevitable or predetermined or could it be modified by our own efforts? If it is the latter, then how is it to be changed? Are we aware of the possibilities for directing our fate?

One idea we are loathe to think about is the possibility that we by our own choices are responsible for the direction our history has taken us. Have we deceived ourselves in some way choosing the less desirable of two possibilities ending up with what our history *has* been rather than a better what *could* have been?

We have certain beliefs, attitudes and values often taking them for a fixed reality rather than something we are responsible for having created, a worldview that might be causing a less than pleasant experience. Take the belief in American exceptionalism for example:

Myth 1: There is something superior about American exceptionalism
Myth 2: The U.S. behaves better than other nations do
Myth 3: America's success is due to its special genius
Myth 4: The U.S. is responsible for most of the good in the world
Myth 5: God is on our side[2]

The first myth

The irony built into America's history is the contrast between reality and illusion. We are not the only nation to think we are superior (exceptional). "The British thought they were bearing the 'white man's burden,' while French colonialists invoked *la mission civilisatrice* to justify their empire. Portugal [Spain's chief competitor in the New World during the time of Columbus], whose imperial activities were hardly distinguished, believed it was promoting a certain *missao civilizadora*. Even many of the officials of the former Soviet Union genuinely believed they were leading the world toward a socialist utopia despite the many cruelties that communist rule inflicted."[3]

The second myth

This could be called the "holier than thou myth." Many of us truly believe that we behave better than other great powers and conveniently overlook those behaviors that might suggest otherwise. "Asked recently about an innocent man who had been tortured to death in an American 'black site' in Afghanistan, former Vice President Dick Cheney did not hesitate. 'I'm more concerned,' he said, 'with bad guys who got out and released than I am with a few that, in fact, were innocent.'"4 Compassion is a casualty, or we might say, part of the "collateral damage" attending the behavior of an arrogant American worldview.

All nations and most individuals are unconscious and controlled by their false-self survival strategies and are driven to adopt "survival of the fittest" behaviors. It is then not so ironic that the U.S. has done what it thought it had to do to survive and paid little attention to moral principles, especially where the *other* was concerned.

The third myth

We call this myth "just plain ole dumb luck." It was not God (manifest destiny) or especially intelligent men and women in leadership positions who elevated America to our position as the leader of the free world. During our early history the powerful European nations were busy fighting one another, giving us some breathing space to get established, which enabled us to play them off against one another in our foreign policy. Our location, half a world away from European conflicts, insulated us from the madness of nation state competition.

Taking advantage of the preoccupation of the European nations with each other's ambitions the timing was right to ignore British demands that colonists not cross the Appalachians in 1763; pick up the Louisiana Purchase from a cash-strapped Napoleon; bully Spain and later Mexico into surrendering territory; and grab Alaska from a clueless Russia. Perhaps the greatest piece of good luck was that the continent was rich in natural resources, free for the taking from indigenous peoples too few in numbers to resist.

The fourth myth

Yes, Americans have done good things in the world, just not enough that we can ignore the times when we didn't. We have fought unnecessary wars wasting thousands of American lives and trillions of dollars, not even bothering to count the lives of the not so exceptional *others* (again the collateral damage) nor to acknowledge the devastation wrought to their cultures.

The war in Vietnam was rationalized by the non-existent "domino theory" based on a non-existent monolithic communism. The hubris of the American military in the Iraq war which predicted being greeted with flowers and parades upon the liberation of Baghdad collapsed when instead they experienced RPGs (rocket-propelled grenades) and IEDs (improvised explosive devices). The false self and its childish need for affection and esteem create a trap for the bloated machismo of the American male.

The fifth myth

Ronald Reagan supported the idea that the U.S. was part of a divine plan, a more appropriate theme for a Hollywood movie than a mature nation's identity. He once quoted Pope Pius XII saying "Into the hands of America God has placed the destinies of an afflicted mankind."[5] President Bush in 2004 displaying more "delusions of grandeur" than calm mature leadership said, "We have a calling from beyond the stars to stand for freedom."[6]

Americans will experience a very special freedom indeed when they escape the bonds of the bogus P-B story which hides the truth that all human beings in the global village are exactly alike. The irony of our history is that by working so hard to deny our selfish pursuit of plenty, pleasure and power, we destroy any chance that we will experience our *truly* exceptional True self.

We have not chosen the healthiest worldview (story) and as a consequence are stuck with an identity that drives behavior that is self destructive. How should we be behaving? What should we have learned from our past behaviors?

Speaking of the experience of life as a quest, Joseph Campbell describes what our mythology (not history) has revealed to those awake enough to experience it. "The ultimate aim of the quest must be neither release nor ecstasy for oneself, but the wisdom and the power to serve others."[7]

Ghosts

Where your concentration goes, your energy flows and that's what grows.

When most of us are so used to seeing ghosts, we should begin to suspect as did a certain prince in a kingdom long, long ago that something is rotten in Denmark. We can't create a functional community in America let alone hope to help our neighbors create them abroad when we are all freaked out by specters under our beds. This deeply "imbedded" anxiety is universal in the global village; a common component of the human worldview. Do these chain-rattling shufflers emitting low guttural moans actually have anything to do with human behavior? Well, let's take a look.

The torment occasioned by Hamlet imagining his father's ghost had him create havoc within the walls of Elsinore castle. Imagine how we would all react to flesh and blood "ghosts" threatening *us*. In truth, we don't have to imagine; we are all living within our own version of an Elizabethan tragedy. The ghosts in question are of course the *other* and they are strictly a figment of our imagination; they don't in fact exist, they are projections of our own neuroses and worldview content.

These ghosts have been around as long as we have so they have a history. Let's start there. We are all ghosts to someone. To some people we are "different" in a particular way—skin color, religion, age, ethnicity, sexual preference, dress, language, mannerisms, college degrees, the list goes on and on—and we are therefore the *other* to them just as they are the *other* to us. We all have someone we are afraid of and there are those who are afraid of us. It doesn't take much to be perceived as a ghostly *other*. All of these anxiety-producing differences, sadly, are superficial, they have no substance; "they" are not really "there." The differences are specter-like visual and auditory sensations.

The imagined existence of the *other* is doubly sad because as long as we continue to imagine the presence of these phantasmagoria, truly compassionate human interactions will be impossible. In spending so much of our energy in destroying that which doesn't exist, we will destroy ourselves and create a massive amount of suffering in the process. The record of this self-destruction is clear to those who have the courage to look at it.

One curious thing about the link between the ghosts of the past and today's ghosts is that they are often the same. Ghosts have a particular resilience. They don't seem to die. Why is that? It has to do with the origin of our ghosts. Ghosts emerge from the sensation or what is often called the affection/esteem energy center of the false-self survival strategy. What a mouthful! In short, our false self is looking for a way to feel good about itself and also for someone else on whom to project (unload) those unconscious traits it does not like. So we have the crazy human dynamic of working hard to keep our ghosts alive so they can travel through history with us as convenient carriers (scape ghosts) of our self-loathing. I know, I know, that sounds like a lot of hooey but keep reading and see if the following examples don't make sense.

Native Americans as the *Other*

In the late 1700s the Rev. Junipero Serra established a chain of church missions along the coast of California. His goal was to bring Christianity to the American Indians. The result was an assault upon the *other* living on the frontier of colonial Spain in the New World. "The Indians were forced to shed their language, dress, religion, food, and marriage customs. Thousands died from exposure to European diseases to which they had no immunity. Of the approximately 310,000 Indians in 1769 in what is now California, only one-sixth remained a hundred years later, according to a University of California historian."[1]

Pope Francis plans to canonize Father Serra (2015) putting him closer to sainthood. Apparently Catholics believe the myth that thousands of Indians were Christianized and civilized by the kindness and compassion of the missionaries.

History betrays the myopia of the false self where in the retelling of the story of the missions, the *other* disappears. Robert M. Senkewicz co-author of *California, Indians and the*

Transformation of a Missionary, reveals American history to be a P-B narrative. "The way contemporary missions are presented, the Indians are absent."[2] Their ghosts, however, still wander the halls of our history whispering the true motives of the Church's pursuit of God, Glory and Gold.

The scapegoats of the Church's very dark shadow remain devastated by its projection over 200 years later. "American Indians are victims of violent crime at a rate more than double that of the rest of the population, according to the first [1999] nationwide survey the federal government has done on the subject."[3]

The history of the *other* in the U.S. is often about being used in the pursuit of plenty, pleasure and power. Three men saw a band of Cheyenne and Arapaho Indians camped on Big Sandy Creek not far from Denver. They saw it as an opportunity to further their respective goals. The encampment contained mostly women, children and elderly men.

Colonel John Chivington and his troops arrived at the camp on November 29, 1864 and saw Chief Black Kettle raise an American flag and a small white flag as he had been told to do to indicate that his was a friendly encampment. "Women and children were scalped, fingers cut off to get the rings on them, a Lt. Col. cut off ears of all he came across. A squaw ripped open and a child taken from her. Little children shot while begging for their lives and all the indignities shown their bodies that was heard of."[4] This was the eyewitness description of Army Lt. Joe A. Cramer in a letter found in 2000, which stated that the "officer in command should be hung."[5]

Chivington later boasted in an appearance before Congress that his men had killed 500 or 600 Indians and lied saying "I saw no dead children."[6] Treatment of the *other* is not an image easy to look at it but if we turn away from the truth we will never find it.

The false-self's behaviors are well-known to us and are revealed by its ambitions. The territorial governor, John Evans, wanted the Indians removed so the Union Pacific Railroad would come to Denver, encouraging commerce and driving up land values. William Byers knew the story would sell copies of his *Rocky Mountain News*. Colonel Chivington was running for Congress. The moans of the ghosts of elderly men, of the women and children, can still be heard above the slow, steady trickle of Big Sandy Creek.

Beginning under President Andrew Jackson, Indians of the Five Civilized Tribes living in the Southeastern U.S. were forcibly marched to the Indian Territory in what is now Oklahoma. The family of Mary Basquez was given forty acres which now has six oil wells on it. She should be entitled to royalties from the wells but remember, she is the *other*.

She lives in a little house in which she can't look out the window to see her land. "The windows are boarded up because she is unable to afford basic home improvements ... 'It makes me so mad. I see all the oil they're taking away, but then I get a statement for $5 or less.'"[7]

Again, notice how the false self finds a way to exploit the Native American *other*. The trust which issues Mary's $5 check dates from the 1887 General Allotment Act when reservations in Oklahoma were broken up and Native Americans were given 80 to 160 acres each. How did the "whites" get their hands on these assets? First, declaring that the American Indians were incapable of managing their own land, thereby making the government a trustee for many of the land owners.

Secondly, leasing the American Indian parcels to oil, gas, timber, grazing and mining interests. Thirdly, to achieve the payoff or end result which was likely intended all along: "Rather than making Indians prosperous, by most accounts, the allotment system destroyed tribal wealth and led to Indians losing two-thirds of the land."[8] One day Mary's ghost will furiously shuffle across her dusty 40 acres continuing to curse the Bureau of Indian Affairs.

African Americans as the *Other*

History evolves, less because new facts are discovered than because the false self has changing needs to use history to justify its delusional identity. Nothing illustrates this better than the curious behavior of Southerners who are still fighting the Civil War 150 years after Appomattox. It works both ways in that pro-Northern sympathizers are also always "discovering" new facts to bolster their biased view of history.

We begin with the ever-controversial "Sherman's march to the sea." A recently placed historical marker in Atlanta says that 62,000 soldiers under Sherman's command devastated "Atlanta's industrial and business districts" and relates how "contrary to popular myth, Sherman's troops primarily destroyed only property used for waging war—railroads, train depots, factories, cotton gins and warehouses."[9] Stephen Davis, author of *What the Yankees Did to Us: Sherman's Bombardment and Wrecking of Atlanta* said of the marker: "They're bending over backward to give Sherman a whitewash that he does not deserve."[10]

Longtime leader of the Sons of Confederate Veterans Chapter in Georgia, revealing his long-simmering resentment, tries to keep a long-dead scapegoat alive. "How they can justify saying anything other than that he's Billy the Torch, I don't know."[11] Notice the present-tense reaction.

The false self does not find it easy or even possible to let old (sometimes *very* old) wounds heal when it feels it's "self-esteem" has been disrespected. James C. Cobb, a professor at the University of Georgia and former president of the Southern Historical Association gives his explanation of why old grievances are so passionately nursed and kept alive. "The old stereotype is a long way from disappearing. There's this sort of instinctive sense of Sherman embodying the whole Yankee cause and the presumed vindictiveness and unrelenting harshness that the white South was subjected to."[12]

Sherman biographer John F. Marszalek sees the old soldier as perhaps more sophisticated in his wartime strategy than he really was. "His whole concept was psychological warfare. He did such a good job getting into people's minds, he's still there in many ways."[13] Grieving Southerners have ghosts in their minds alright but it isn't that of William Tecumseh Sherman.

But, of course, it wasn't only northern generals that received most of the projections of the white southern false self. White southerners had two favorite scapegoats, Sherman and their own neighbors. Jason Sokol chronicled the story of white southerners coping with the civil rights era imagining grievances kept alive today.

The African American is targeted everywhere in the U.S. historically and today. For example, despite his status in the world of baseball, Jackie Robinson and his family were unwelcome as homeowners in the suburbs of Northeastern cities. Sokol, in his new book *All Eyes Are Upon Us: Race Politics From Boston to Brooklyn* writes, "They saw a hero in one black ballplayer but ruin in a thousand black migrants."[14] Fear of chaos joins shame and regret as underlying sources of energy that drive the reactive behavior of the false self.

Jill Leovy is one of those people who today has the courage to look at the truth and she does so in her book *GHETTOSIDE: A True Story of Murder in America*. "African-American males are, as she puts it, 'just 6 percent of the country's population but nearly 40 percent of those murdered.'"[15] As in the case of the tragedy of the Native Americans, this catastrophic injustice is something most of us never see and quickly put out of mind if we happen to read about it. Denial is a basic behavioral trait for almost everyone in P-B, otherwise, how would we sleep at night.

In a ghetto like Watts in Los Angeles with a high homicide rate among the *other*, one can literally "get away with murder." In a 13-year period 2,672 black males where murdered and a suspect was arrested in only 38 percent of those cases.

Among the casualties of denial is truth, and in the Simple Reality Project truth is important, it has a high priority. Let us have more truth—less denial, more response—less reaction, more compassion and in turn less fear. If we don't we will continue to have places like Watts. Leovy writes "Where the criminal justice system fails to respond vigorously to violent injury and death homicide becomes endemic … [the] system's failure to catch killers effectively made black lives cheap."[16] No! The failure is in seeing African Americans as the *other* that makes black lives cheap and expendable.

Jews as the *Other*

It is critically important that we give the elimination of the illusion of the *other* the highest priority because it's potential for catastrophe is so great. For example, mass murders have already happened many times throughout history with collective projections onto collective *others*. The collective shadow when manipulated into paranoia is easily mesmerized and is then capable of unimaginable and horrific behavior; but we don't have to imagine, history shows recent examples of this mass hysteria.

These horrors are hard to imagine for most of us. All the more reason we must try to understand them. "The crucial elements are the political leaders' decision to commit genocide, the willing participation of a large population of perpetrators, the sympathy of an even broader civilian population—in the case of the Holocaust, principally ordinary Germans, but also many other Europeans—and, above all, the ideology that motivates them all to believe that annihilating the targeted people is necessary and right."[17]

Sometimes the leaders of mass projections which become mass exterminations are so abhorrent that the leaders have to conceal what is happening from the very people who support it and enable them to pretend it isn't happening or to at least engage in the charade of denial. "The Nazi leadership created death factories not for expeditious reasons, but to distance the killers from their victims."[18] Nevertheless, most of us, because we have a false self, are capable of aiding and abetting these insidious schemes with rationalizations that work for us.

The worst thing we can do *vis-à-vis* the *other* is to deny reality with unwarranted optimism because then we stop looking for causes and solutions. Milan Salomonovic, 81, spent several weeks in Auschwitz as a child and knows first-hand the experience of the *other*. "'When the war was over, everybody was convinced it would be the end of the war and of anti-Semitism. People simply have not learned the lesson of Auschwitz,' he said."[19]

But the lesson we all need to learn is much more profound than the delusions surrounding the Holocaust. That lesson is about the *other* and our bogus identities determined by our P-B narrative.

We tend to delude ourselves and think we believe in ideals that are only given lip service. Daniel Jonah Goldhagen the author of *Hitler's Willing Executioners: Ordinary Germans and the Holocaust* and *The Devil That Never Dies: The Rise and Threat of Global Anti-Semitism* believes that the Nazis "sought to overturn the fundamentals of Western civilization, including its core notion of a common humanity."[20] There is no notion of a common humanity (Oneness) in the global village and NEVER HAS BEEN in any civilization in the West or the East. History gives the lie to that ideal which amounts to a dangerous self-deception.

In Rwanda in 1994, the Hutu seeing the Tutsis as the hated *other* slaughtered 800,000 of them using mainly machetes, knives and clubs. No modern technology was needed to exceed the daily rate achieved by the Germans in exterminating Jews. The basic psychological motivation for extermination, ethnic cleansing or racial purification is the same despite these different labels. We each create and carry a ghost within which has been traveling with us throughout our history and we are the only one who can exorcize that ghost.

The Mirrors of History

There are a couple of ways to "reflect" on the "reflections" of history. When standing in the amusement park "funhouse" hall of mirrors (P-B), the images of history range from comic distortions to the more common tragically grotesque. Only the undistorted images seen from the perspective of P-A (the conventional, non-distorting mirror) accurately reflect what happened in the past. Revisiting some recent distorted historical images we will notice the difference in how they appeared then and how we can see them more clearly in the context of Simple Reality.

When the false self looks into the mirror at past events and current events, it sees the reflections twisted and stretched by its own craving and anxiety; what it *wants* history to be *not* what has actually happened.

One source of the "Ugly American" reflected in the eyes of people around the world would be America's behavior toward other nations. Beginning in the 19th century it could be said that the U.S. had an interventionist foreign policy. A paranoid collective false self is not going to be able to mind its own business and is bound to offend its neighbors.

One behavior common among paranoid neighbors is spying on one another. Lack of trust means an insatiable curiosity about what the people next door (today that means anywhere in the world) are up to. The behavior of the C.I.A. in the recent past will reflect this virtually universal defensive worldview.

However, as we shall see, the Central Intelligence Agency has been anything but "intelligent." A "spy" organization that lacks intelligence, and more importantly one that lacks awareness of what drives human behavior, is very dangerous. The C.I.A. has created chaos around the planet and contributed to damaging the nation it purports to protect. Now for some historical facts to back up what to some may be an outlandish assertion. Here are some images reflected in the mirrors of history.

National security and foreign policy institutions should have mutually supportive goals. A healthy foreign policy would be in the best long-term interest of the nation. Two brothers just walked into our funhouse and their images reflected in the mirrors would be comical if they weren't so repulsive.

Many Americans have a high opinion of themselves (American exceptionalism) but is that opinion shared beyond our borders? Apparently not in the eyes of book reviewer Adam LeBor or Stephen Kinzer, author of *The Brothers: John Foster Dulles, Allen Dulles and Their Secret World War*. LeBor begins his review of Kinzer's book with this sentence: "Anyone wanting to know why the United States is hated across much of the world need look no further than this book."[1] If the image of the U.S. is ugly in "much of the world" perhaps we might want to see if we can bring it into a clearer focus with the goal of changing the behaviors that tarnish how we appear to others.

John Foster Dulles served as Secretary of State from 1953-1959 and his brother Allen Dulles ran the C.I.A. from 1953-1961. (Dwight D. Eisenhower was president and Richard Nixon VP from 1953-1961. Surprised?) Before the Dulles brothers entered public service they played key roles for decades greasing the connections between the corporate world and American foreign policy.

For example, John Foster Dulles played a central role in channeling funds from the U.S. to Nazi Germany in the 1930s. "Indeed, his friendship with Hjalmar Schacht, the Reichsbank president and Hitler's minister of economics, was crucial to the rebuilding of the German economy. Sullivan and Cromwell [the firm where both brothers were lawyers and partners] floated bonds for Krupp A.G., the arms manufacturer, and also worked for I.G. Farben, the chemicals conglomerate that later manufactured Zyklon B, the gas used to murder millions of Jews."[2]

We can see how a short-sighted false self lacks the awareness to respond to the long-term best interest of U.S. security and foreign policy. The security energy centers of the Dulles brothers, their zeal in making a buck, aided Hitler's Third

Reich and the expression of Adolph Hitler's power energy center. They would have been well advised had they any notion of future public service to observe the reflection of Hitler's distorted psyche by reading *Mein Kampf*.

Human survival strategies run amok continued on a global scale following World War II. President Truman, not as obsessed with the *other* as many Washington politicians, dissolved the O.S.S. which was later reborn as the C.I.A. Allen Dulles, representing the J. Henry Schroeder Banking Corporation probably began to see that he could do a big favor for one of his bank's clients, the Anglo-Iranian Oil Company, by becoming director of the C.I.A.

Mohammed Mossadegh was the leader of Iran in 1953 when the Iranian Parliament voted to nationalize Iran's oil industry. The first step was to cancel a contract that was said to be "the largest overseas development project in modern history."[3] Dulles and his buddies in the world of finance could not afford to let that happen.

There is more than a little irony found in the worldview reflected by the American foreign-policy-funhouse. For example, the Dulles brothers' images can be said to reveal Manichaen-like monsters. The Dulles' images were ironic in that Manichaeism was a third century dualistic Persian philosophy. The Dulles brothers appeared to have a dual but contradictory allegiance to both the U.S. and their "free enterprise" employers. In truth they didn't know who they were and a clear mirror reflection revealed that they were lackeys of their distorted and unconscious pseudo-identities.

The madness in the chaotic funhouse is that American institutions enabled the Third Reich in building a war machine which then took six years to destroy. This was soon followed by the C.I.A and American foreign policy creating yet another long-term enemy that still bedevils our most clever government officials. We ultimately drove a Communist-hating Muslim nation into the arms of the Soviet Union. This brilliant move was the result again of pure greed. The C.I.A. engineered the overthrow of Mossadegh replacing him with the American puppet, Shah

Mohammed Reza Pahlavi. The U.S. in the meantime has managed to turn the entire Middle East into a cauldron of chaos. It all started with those two Dulles boys who seemed to reflect a healthy identity at the time.

The images in the funhouse of history are wildly distorted and discombobulating but there is a certain sameness to them when viewed over time. A certain type of distortion seems to be repeated when closely studied. Most students of American history don't seem to notice this ever-present prototypical dysfunctional behavior.

However, as time passes there is always the possibility that the distorted images all too often reflecting fear and panic may appear more normal. The C.I.A. is still up to expressing its Chicken Little worldview imagining every cloud on the horizon is a bit of falling sky. Because of ineffective methods of interrogation (think torturing) at Guantanamo Bay, we should wince at the expression of our collective identity which may *seem* to have devolved from American exceptionalism to American shame.

"Years before the release in December [2014] of a Senate Intelligence Committee report detailing the C.I.A.'s use of torture and deceit in its detention program, an internal review by the agency found that the C.I.A. had repeatedly overstated the value of intelligence gained during the brutal interrogation of some of the detainees."[4] This was an internal report which we would suspect might have pulled some punches and that the truth just may be a bit more grim and damning.

"The Bush administration opened with a second Pearl Harbor [9-11], ended with a second Great Crash [The Great Recession of 2008], and contained a second Vietnam [Afghanistan/Iraq] in the middle."[5] Does history repeat itself? It is worse than that—it never changes—so it doesn't matter whether we read it forward or backward.

If we spend enough time in the funhouse bedazzled by the flowing images, we begin to take them for reality and the disorientation can make us doubt what we are seeing. It fails to make sense after a while and the mirrors begin to come closer and the panic of claustrophobia can cause us to doubt our judgment. What is real and what is the reflection?

Can you identify this president by the nonsensical reflections dancing around him?[f] "Then a president finds his job has shrunk to cajoling a recalcitrant Congress, exhorting an indifferent public and reconciling warring factions within an administration, where he takes the blame for actions over which had no control and that he probably would have opposed had he been given any advance notice of them."[6]

For some of us the whole funhouse spectacle can be a little much and for others they not only see bizarre and distorted images swirling around them, they are certain that UFO's have visited the earth piloted by creatures that will make the mirror-emanating people seem tame by comparison. For a few of us the only solution would seem to be a subterranean refuge—flee, flee before it's too late.

We could call this underground escape hatch the "silo solution." There are 72 abandoned Atlas-F missile sites, 10 stories deep, concrete tubes capable of withstanding a nuclear strike. They not only offer protection from extraterrestrials and out-of-control mirror images but are a refuge from hurricanes, tornadoes, radiation and yes, zombies if it should come to that. For you survivalists, these structures would seem ideal.

Larry Hall has developed one of the sites and it seems to be a success. "Mr. Hall transformed one silo in Kansas into luxury 'survival condos,' with a pool and spa, theater, shooting range, rock-climbing wall, dog park and five different power sources. Also on hand is hydroponic food, biometric locks and a minor surgery center should residents need to ride out an apocalypse. (The site is designed to sustain 70 people for at least five years.)"[7]

---

[f] President Barack Obama

No mention of any funhouse mirrors in the silos, but then most of us have had our fill of those reflections. Any more of these images and we will all be heading for the silos like rats fleeing a sinking ship.

History: A Story, Your Story, Our Story And *The* Story

Are we saying that knowledge of history, however subjective, has no value? No! Knowledge of any kind in P-A is neutral. Knowledge can be helpful if we know what it means, if we know how to interpret it. The false self in P-B is incapable of using knowledge in a profound way because it lacks the ability to distinguish between reality and illusion. For example, let's go back to colonial America when Big Tobacco was "little tobacco."

It is not what we discover and invent that determines our fate but rather how and why we use it. During the early years of the Jamestown venture, a gentleman John Rolfe experimented with raising tobacco. Up until that time the colony was on shaky ground and was not returning a profit to its investors. "His experiments with the raising of tobacco led to the establishment of that crop as the foundation of Virginia."[1] All that remained was to convince the people back home that the use of tobacco was hip and pleasurable. Given the hunger of the false self for another distraction from suffering, that was not difficult.

In a relatively short time tobacco became an object of craving and grew to be and remains one of the scourges of humanity. It was soon Virginia's largest export, attracted thousands of colonists to become planters and along with other crops became a major impetus for the growth of slavery throughout much of the South. Seeking the illusion of pleasure we often fall into the trap of habit. "Cigarette smoking surged at the beginning of the 20th century, and into the mid 1970's, about 40 percent of American adults were smokers, and they could smoke everywhere they wanted—in restaurants, on buses and airplanes, in workplaces and college classrooms, in their cars with the windows up and their children in the passenger seats."[2]

It's not as if Americans didn't have the knowledge about the harmful effects of tobacco, it's more that most smokers didn't *want* to know and were quick to deny the implications of what they learned or inadvertently discovered. "A Johns Hopkins researcher reported in 1938 that smokers did not live as long as non-smokers ... In 1964, the U.S. surgeon general, Luther L. Terry, issued a landmark report. It linked smoking and cancer and set in motion decades of measures that deeply cut into smoking rates and tobacco's profits and [political] influence, beginning, first, with Congress's passing measures that required health warnings on cigarette packages and later banning cigarette advertising on the radio and TV ... In 1998, they [Big Tobacco] agreed to pay $206 billion to settle a lawsuit brought by the attorneys general of 46 states, who were seeking compensation for costs to the public related to smoking-related illnesses."[3]

It took about 50 years to reduce rates of tobacco consumption from 40 percent to today's (2014) 18 percent. To change ingrained habits involves the changing of the context or story. What is socially acceptable has to be made socially unacceptable. Changing the collective story in a culture results in a change of identity and people who quit smoking did so in part because they could no longer see themselves as smokers. "Our story" becomes "my story." This is one of the ways that history unfolds.

Don't expect Big Tobacco to go away until we learn to cope with the desires of the false-self sensation center. As long as there are sleepwalkers desperate to escape their neurotic anxieties there will be a market for new generations of tobacco products. "Reynolds American Inc. is launching a cigarette that heats tobacco rather than burning it, hoping to capitalize on the growing appetite for alternatives to traditional smokes."[4]

This latest cigarette follows on the heels of the E-cigarette or vapor cigarette already marketed to young people. "'It needed the mass presence of vapor products to open up an experience base that smokers understood,' said J. Brice O'Brien, head of consumer marketing for the maker of Camel and Pall Mall cigarettes."[5]

What if a town wanted to protect its young people by outlawing all tobacco products? Don't underestimate the ability of the easily offended false self to rationalize how tobacco use was a basic American freedom. Yes, like rapid-fire assault rifles.

The Board of Health in Westminster, Massachusetts (November 2014) voted to ban the sale of all tobacco products in their town, the first town in the U.S. to try this. One would think that the British were coming again in the state where Lexington and Concord girded up their loins to resist foreign invasion. But this time it's not the freedom from taxation that is being defended, it's the freedom to commit suicide.

Andrea Crete chairwoman of the Board of Health said, "The Board of Health permitting these establishments to sell these dangerous products that, when used as directed, kill 50 percent of its users, ethically goes against our public health mission."[6]

What about protecting the young people of the community? Again, Andrea Crete quoting from a report from the surgeon general, said that "youth who shop at least twice a week in stores that sell tobacco are 64 percent more likely to start smoking than those who do not."[7]

The majority of citizens in Westminster, however, later proved that they were more concerned with their right to buy tobacco products than their health or the health of their children. This we recognize as an extreme reaction of the false self. Dr. Corey Saltin, a lung specialist in private practice near Westminster said he "understood concerns about free choice but that people who are subjected to secondhand smoke have rights too. 'This ban is going to happen somewhere, sometime,' Dr. Saltin predicted. 'But probably not in Westminster.'"[8]

Most of us have many deeply ingrained habits that are unhealthy. Some destructive habits are part of our identity as individuals, or some a part of our identity as a member of a nation or community. The beliefs (smoking is cool), attitudes (it's nobody's business if I want to smoke) and values (the choice to smoke should be a fundamental freedom in a democracy) explain the stories of many people who rationalize the behaviors driven by their mostly unconsciously held false-self survival strategy.

The problem that some of us fail to see is that all individuals in a community are connected and any individual's behavior ultimately affects the rest of us. A successful community is not one where the individual is free to do their own thing, but rather one in which the highest value is sharing and caring for one another. The current dilemma related to global warming brings out two different stories or worldviews expressed by Washington politicians concerning how to react to this threat.

"A variety of polls show that a majority of American voters now believe that climate change is occurring, are worried about it, and support candidates who back policies to stop it."[9] In other words, the majority of Americans give policies that protect the environment a high priority.

"But Republicans are betting that despite the polls, they can make the case that regulations to cut greenhouse pollution will result in the loss of jobs and hurt the economy."[10] In other words, Republicans are appealing to the more immediate need of the security center of the collective American survival strategy. The story of the individual's need for employment trumps the story of the human community as a whole, or the softer message of long-term planning is drowned out by the blare of the short-term anxiety many individuals have. Two different stories leading to two different behaviors.

The role that the *other* played in the story of colonial Jamestown had the colonists projecting on the indigenous people and vice versa with tragic consequences that remain a part of America's story today just as the story of the slave as *other* working in the tobacco fields impacts American identities today.

The past is never dead. It's not even past.
   William Faulkner

"For example, counties in America that had a higher proportion of slaves in 1860 are still more unequal today, according to a scholarly paper published in 2010. The authors called this a 'persistent effect of slavery.'"[11]

Corporations and companies helped perpetuate a form of slavery long after the Civil War. "Douglas Blackmon won a Pulitzer Prize for his devastating history, *Slavery by Another Name*, that recounted how U.S. Steel and other American corporations used black slave labor well into the 20th century, through 'convict leasing.' Blacks would be arrested for made-up offenses such a 'vagrancy' and then would be leased to companies as slave laborers.'"[12]

In 2014 The Walk Free Foundation, a human rights group based in Australia, examining 167 countries, found that India had 14.3 million people who were victims of slavery (36 million globally). But surely slavery today has finally been eliminated in the U.S. Guess again. "About 60,100 people are exploited as forced laborers in the U.S."[13]

Those who see history for what it is, a story, may come to realize that it has always been thus. We get up each morning and create fundamentally the same story as we did the day before which becomes "our story" and we expect it to change but it never has—and it won't—until we admit that we have grown weary of the old story, the old identity and the old catastrophic behaviors.

"Hunger came to the countryside, to the towns, to Paris, it was sharp enough in the masses to overcome tradition, reverence, and fear, and to provide an instrument for the aims and brains of well-fed men. The dykes of law and custom and piety broke, and the Revolution began."[14] For some, chaos is catastrophe, for those with a lust for power, it is an opportunity. For those of us who understand that history in P-B never changes, we know it to be an illusion and we know how to escape with our heads still on our shoulders, but most people today are headed for some version of the guillotine.

History: His-story And Her-story

The dogmas of the quiet past are inadequate to the stormy present ... As our case is new, so we must think anew and act anew.
        In Lincoln's address to Congress
        in December 1862

Those who have read even a couple of Simple Reality essays must have learned the importance of the distinction between the story we call illusion (P-B) and the story we call Simple Reality (P-A). To understand the "Big Picture" of the human condition through time, the story is all-important. One of the most tragic and disturbing stories in human history is "her-story." Women got off to an inauspicious beginning with the Christian story of Eve's insubordination or "immorality" and have suffered the slings and arrows of myth ever since. We needn't slog through history to analyze and prepare to make amends for the treatment of women, we just need the courage to look at reality today and "fix it."

In fact, *all* of "his-story" and "her-story" is present today and staring us in the face. Neither men nor women are going to escape relating to each other in a dysfunctional way without a deeper understanding of how we are all profoundly alike, facing the same basic identity which is the origin of all our suffering.

How can a species survive without women and children? And yet, women and children today around the world are the least respected, the least protected, and receive less compassion from the men who control our societies than those men show to each other. Sounds outrageous, and yet we must keep our attention focused—remember—the courage to look at reality.

One of the largest groups receiving projections as the *other* today makes up half the populations of India, Egypt, Norway and the U.S. Notice how the differences in the four cultural stories or contexts influences the treatment of women in these four societies.

Men project their fear on women as the *other*. Yes, many men are afraid of women virtually everywhere but you don't have to accept that observation to see how in these next four stories "his-story" is linked to "her-story" and how the P-B narrative is causing them both unnecessary suffering.

Perhaps you think we might be overstating the case in, say, western societies today (2014). But in fact, we might even go further by saying that certain animals are treated better than women. "The Royal Society for the Prevention of Cruelty to Animals was founded in 1824, nine years before the British Empire abolished slavery. Today a donkey sanctuary in Devon attracts more donations per year than the three most prominent British Charities dealing with violence against women combined."[1] Apparently, an ass beating an ass would attract more censors than an ass beating a woman. More about the asses in question in a moment.

When it comes to expressing the power energy center of the false self, it seems that women have not been able to acquire the degree of control over the political and economic systems that men have. Even when those women are advocating for children, the American male does not seem too concerned.

Could it be that women follow the lead of the men rather than their own self-interest? "Congress has been debating early education programs for more than 40 years and it has hardly made a dent. A great many of our employers don't bother to make jobs more family-friendly; they don't even bother to make modest arrangements to accommodate their pregnant workers. Everybody thinks this is extremely unfortunate [oh really], but almost nobody does anything about it because there is not a lot of political or financial reward for siding with working mothers."[2] Political or financial reward for whom? Ahhhh, now you're catching on.

Speaking of women in the workplace, "her-storically" a recent phenomenon, a personal story illustrates that workers are equal, but some are more equal than others and we can guess which those are. Jessica Stensrud has been dealing with those barnyard pigs who think they are "better than" for some time in the workplace. "I graduated from Carnegie Mellon University in biological sciences (pre-med program) and was a violin student of Itzhak Perlman. I have always had to fight like hell to be taken as an equal either in music or in I.T. Now that I am almost 65, there are still more battles—age *and* sex discrimination—clearly present at my current job."³

Women have a right to equality in the workplace and also support in providing our society with the incomparable blessing of children. They have no such luck on either score. Remember, discrimination against women is a power issue no matter where it occurs and it is the men who feel threatened. Do we mean that the hairy-chested guy in the buffalo skin with the 40-pound club protecting the cave entrance is frightened? Yep! That's him.

Peggy Young, a driver for UPS, had an accident that limited her ability to lift heavy packages and probably would have been assigned "light duty" or another type of work but then she became pregnant and was told by her doctor not to lift packages over 20 pounds. UPS put her on unpaid medical leave. Alas, she was cursed with wanting to bring a child into the world.⁴

As we all have heard in recent times, women are finding discrimination in the work place and also are bumping up against it in their religions. We thought some good news would be refreshing at this point. "The Church of England overturned centuries of tradition on Monday (December 2014) with a final vote allowing women to become bishops, with the first appointment possible by Christmas."⁵

This same measure was defeated in 2012. "But Archbishop Welby, the spiritual leader of the church and the global Anglican Communion, who supported the vote from the start, had warned fellow church leaders this year that the public would find the exclusion of women 'almost incomprehensible.'"⁶ Speaking of the incomprehensible, let us continue.

Let's move on to some other aspects of "her-story" that we find hard to believe. We mentioned earlier that Britain abolished slavery in the first half of the 19th century. Unfortunately, *abolishing* slavery was not the same as *ending* it. The current statistics are heart-rending and involve a predominance of females, both women and children.

The 2014 Global Report on Trafficking in Persons revealed that most victims are female and that one in three trafficking victims is a child. One in three! "While sexual exploitation remains the predominant reason for trafficking, victims are also increasingly being used for forced labor."[7] Slavery is still found in every part of the world and perpetrators seldom suffer consequences for this most heinous crime.

It is perhaps shocking for those who think the forward movement of history involves *progress* to learn of the increase in slavery in the 21st century. The next abusive treatment of girls that will merit our outrage is as difficult to believe as selling them into slavery. "UNICEF estimates that of the 125 million women worldwide who have undergone genital cutting in the 29 countries where it is most prevalent—mostly in Africa and the Middle East—one in five lives in Egypt."[8]

What is genital cutting or genital mutilation? "According to the World Health Organization, it 'comprises all procedures that involve partial or total removal of the external female genitalia or other injury to the female genital organs for nonmedical reasons.' The procedure has no health benefits. We hack away at perfectly healthy parts of our girls' genitals because we're obsessed with female virginity and because women's sexuality is a taboo."[9] The "we" here is the fear-driven male in a culture wherein he seeks power and control over the women in that society.

The male power structure in these societies is not conscious of the underlying motive of power and control and has other "rationales" for this egregious sexual abuse. "This cutting is believed to reduce a girl's sex drive. And families believe their daughters are unmarriageable unless they are cut."[10] We know that the story or paradigm involving beliefs, attitudes and values drives the behavior in a given society and it is the males that "write" that narrative.

The story in question triumphs over so-called historical progress as the statistics on slavery suggest. So it is with genital mutilation. Even though laws were passed in Egypt outlawing the practice it has continued to increase. "'Medicalized' cutting is at 77 percent—up from 55 percent 20 years ago. When I [journalist Mona Eltahawy] interviewed a 53-year-old survivor of the practice in Cairo for a BBC radio documentary about women in the Middle East, she told me, 'It must be carried out, because that's the way to maintain the purity of girls, to make sure that the girl is not out of control. We don't care if it's against the law or if they're trying to stop it. We know doctors who are willing to continue and have done so.'"[11] As we have often said, the story is all-powerful in determining identity and driving behavior.

We in the U.S. might say that males in nations using genital mutilation to assuage their fears of out-of-control females is abhorrent. But we have our own Christian religious conservatives who have similar fears. They think keeping young men and women ignorant gives the church the control they need. Does it work?

"Medicaid spends an average of $12,770 for a birth. Yet we spend only $8 per teenage girl on programs to avoid pregnancy. In financial terms, that's nuts. In human terms, it's a tragedy."[12] We agree with Nicholas Kristof and as we are seeing in this essay, life is suffering in both "his-story" and "her-story" and, tragically, we are not yet finished.

Children should not be brought into the world by accident. It is no exaggeration to say that the global village will overpopulate itself out of existence. The planet's males should fear out-of-control population growth more than the threat of young women having children that many don't want in the first place. LARCs or long-acting reversible contraceptives provided for girls and women who want them will save the nation money and reduce the population of unwanted children who weaken the social fabric. "A study in St. Louis offered free birth control, including LARCs, to sexually active teenagers and found that pregnancy rates for them plunged by more than three-quarters. Abortions fell by a similar rate."[13] The irony is that if foes of abortion want to reduce them, they should support birth control for women. No-brainers are often beyond the grasp of those scared into a fight or flight (denial) reaction.

Comparing America's "story" in this regard to that of our more enlightened cousins abroad we can see that the U.S. is lagging in "historical progress."

- American teenagers become pregnant at a rate of about one a minute.

- Eighty-two percent of births to teenagers in the U.S. are unplanned.

- American and European teenagers seem to be sexually active at roughly similar rates, although Americans may start a bit earlier. But the American teenage birthrate is three times Spain's rate and five times France's, and 15 times Switzerland's.

- Young Americans show a lack of understanding of where babies come from. Among teenagers who unintentionally became pregnant, the Centers for Disease Control and Prevention found that the most cited reason for not using contraception was "I didn't think I could become pregnant."[14]

The old saw "Keep 'em barefoot and pregnant" would seem to be the strategy of the American male in controlling the women who threaten them. An exaggeration? No in fact it should read "Keep them barefoot, pregnant, poor and ignorant" because an unplanned pregnancy can block a woman's education plans, lower her earning potential, reduce her employability, and limit her family to a life of poverty. It's almost as if the American male was conducting war on American women and children.

What about the overpopulation threat? How are the paranoid males dealing with that in a nation where that problem is at a crisis level? What if the males in the government started a sterilization program to benefit the poor? Beware of the male in medical garb who puts on an act of compassion. Check his bank account. Our continuing saga takes us to India where, believe it or not, the male is more terrified of women than the American male.

The structure of the program will quickly reveal its true intention. Women were paid 1400 rupees ($23) for the surgeries. "A 'motivator,' usually a local public health worker, was paid 200 rupees, or about $3.25, to bring a woman to the camp."[15] Those of us in America who invented the assembly line and mass production immediately see the problem here. The more units produced, the higher the profit. Women are not "units," however, and shouldn't be treated as such but try telling that to a greedy surgeon.

"It was not my fault—the administration pressured me to meet targets."[16] What Dr. R. K. Gupta said appears to be true. In much of India, authorities (male of course) aggressively pursue targets and threaten health workers with salary cuts and dismissals. This means that the workers in turn pressure women to undergo sterilization treatments without being provided information on complications or irreversibility. Dr. Gupta, working at breakneck speed, performed 83 surgeries in six hours. Dr. Gupta was arrested in mid-November and charged with culpable homicide when 13 women died after he performed a large number of tubal ligations. Gupta's hubris got the better of him and probably didn't help his case when he bragged, "'These were only 83 operations,' he said, 'I have done 300 on a single day many years ago.'"[17]

Of all the sterilization operations performed in the world, 37 percent are done in India, too fast, as we have seen, with many in unsanitary, assembly-line conditions. "In the 12 months ended in March 2013, 4.6 million Indians were sterilized. Between 2009 and 2012, India's government paid compensation for 568 women who died as a result of the procedures."[18]

Now we return to the U.S. What do a prestigious state university, the U.S. military and one of the most successful American comedians have in common? They have all become embroiled in the alleged crime of rape. These incidents have all come to light in November 2014 but started years, probably many years, ago.

The alleged rape of a coed at a fraternity party at the University of Virginia, the allegations of more than a dozen women that they were drugged and raped by Bill Cosby and the sexual assault charges brought by a 59-year-old Marine Corps veteran are but the latest of a never-ending pattern deeply imbedded in our American culture. Rape is how the male false self seeks to dominate both males and females.

"The fact that there is something fundamentally wrong with the way our society treats women is a proposition on which there is now general agreement."[19] If there were general agreement wouldn't something be done about this widespread tragedy? Is that cultural change, that shift in the American narrative, finally taking place? Don't hold your breath. In fact it's past time for a series of deep breaths just to keep from avoiding despair.

"For all the talk of 'zero tolerance' on campuses, in the military and in the White House of sexual assault, extensive legislation on Capitol Hill has yet to move forward and President Obama has largely stayed out of the fray on the issue."[20] "Critics note that a two-decade-old federal law requiring colleges and universities to disclose information about crime on and around their campuses, including sexual offenses, is rarely enforced."[21] In other words, if women in the U.S. want a change in how they are treated by American males, they will have to become much more pro-active than they have been thus far.

Before behavior will change, values have to change. Which values for example? The University of Virginia was an all-male bastion of privilege until it began to admit women in 1970. The values and behavior of those earlier decades hangs on. The fight song "From Rugby Road to Vinegar Hill" has lyrics that "celebrate drunken excess, sex and, by some accounts sexual assault."[22]

The most frightened males will engage in the most outrageous behavior—blaming the victim. "For decades, officials at Bob Jones University told sexual assault victims that they were to blame for their abuse, and to not report it to the police because doing so would damage their families, churches and the university, according to a long-awaited independent report released Thursday [December 11, 2014]."[23] Like the Catholic Church, fundamentalist Protestant institutions still see the concupiscent Eve when looking at women.

Looking more closely at the American narrative and its history, we see, in a sense that the henhouse and its inhabitants (the females) are being guarded by the fox (the males) and, being hungry, what do we expect the foxes to do? As Nicholas Kristof says, "We are still too passive about sexual violence in our midst, too willing to make excuses, too inclined to perceive shame in being raped. These are attitudes that facilitate violence by creating a protective blanket of silence and impunity. In that sense, we are all enablers."[24] In our society, it's O.K. if a few chickens get eaten.

So far we have seen the words *values* and *attitudes* crop up in our text. If we add the word *belief*, we will have the definition of *worldview*, our story. How do our young men come to believe that it is O.K. to sexually assault the daughters, sister, and mothers, of their community (not to mention the sons, brothers and fathers)? "Too often boys are socialized [taught the worldview of P-B] to see women and girls as baubles, as playthings. The upshot is that rapists can be stunningly clueless, somehow unaware that they have committed a crime or even a *faux pas*."[25] Incredible, but we must *believe* this is happening if there is any chance for behavioral change.

Nowadays women are entering the U.S. military in ever larger numbers. How is it going for them in that most macho of environments? Common sense would say that the military is probably not the best place for a woman to receive training and employment. First of all, women forego the protection of the U.S. Constitution and enter the legal paradigm of the Uniform Code of Military Justice where commanding officers can exercise the role of jury, judge and executioner. Justice in the military wears a blindfold alright, one that doesn't enable "her" to see the female soldier as deserving of impartial treatment.

Even our elected representatives are finding that the military may have too much political support among male politicians to be reformed. In other words when criticized about their behavior, the males in the military close ranks. Senator Kirsten Gillibrand pointed out that the last gender-relations survey from 2012 indicated there had been 26,000 cases of sexual assault, rape and unwanted sexual contact in a year's time. Only one in eight or 3,300 of them were actually reported.

Senator Gillibrand, among other outraged female representatives are trying to uncover the facts. "And so when you speak to the survivors, they'll tell you they won't report because they don't believe the chain of command will do anything or fear witness retaliation. Of the brave souls that did report these crimes, 62 percent were retaliated against. So you have a culture where rapists go free, there's no accountability for sexual assault, there's a climate where everything is shoved under the rug and people are actually punished for reporting sexual assault."[26]

In a rational society economic policies would be designed to benefit both men, women and children. The American economic paradigm reveals a fundamental belief that many people are lazy and cannot be trusted. "It is a simple idea supported by both economic theory and most people's intuition: If welfare benefits are generous and taxes high, fewer people will work. Why bother being industrious, after all, if you can receive a check from the government for sitting around—and if your choice to work means that much of your income will end up in the tax collectors coffers?"[27] Notice how a large and growing segment of the American population becomes the *other* in this narrative. Is this what you believe?

The beliefs, attitudes and values in Scandinavian countries flow from not only a different narrative but a more compassionate and trusting one. The resulting economic policies also support fathers, mothers and children and the *other* is harder to identify in these societies.

"In Scandinavian countries, working parents have the option of heavily subsidized child care. Leave policies make it easy for parents to take off work to care for a sick child. Heavily subsidized public transportation may make it easier for a person in a low-wage job to get to and from work. And free or inexpensive education may make it easier to get the training to move from the unemployment rolls to a job."[28] We could, of course find misogyny in the Scandinavian countries because the male false self is expressing itself there too, but maybe the move toward more humanitarian governmental policies indicates an awakening of the True self. We hope so.

In our brief excursion around the planet looking at the current behavior of men and women in contrasting cultures, we can see how "his-story" and "her-story" have led to varying outcomes in behavior. Planet earth is a part of the totality of all Creation. Regrettably, there is one thing that all of the cultures on our planet have in common. One part of Creation (the human male) self-destructs by making war on another part of Creation (the human female), of which he is an inseparable and mutually dependent part. This behavior is a good definition of insanity. One thing that history *can* tell us, even very recent history, is that something needs to change my dear reader.

CHAPTER 2

THE HUMAN COMMUNITY:
Where We Are Now

Introduction

Sociology can be defined as the study of human social behavior, especially the study of the origins, organization, institutions, and development of human society. Human society on this planet today means P-B.

Simple Reality has sociology as a dominant focus when it comes to analyzing the health of the human community. The best way to diagnose how a community is faring is to look at how the people in that community behave. Sounds simple and it is but unfortunately policy makers who are charged with prescribing after the diagnosis is made have to make their judgments in the context of a highly dysfunctional practice. For example, it's as if Washington politicians are prescribing aspirin for a diseased liver.

Washington doesn't seem to have much respect for sociology even though it could tell them a lot about the most pressing problems in the U.S. Disintegrating families, criminals resistant to rehabilitation, failing educational institutions, an aging population draining limited resources, religions offering delusional narratives, divisive immigration policies, poverty and growing inequality are a few of the challenges we could look at in this chapter. Washington politicians will look at these issues also but they will not understand what they are seeing.

For example, President Obama's "My Brother's Keeper" initiative to combat problems afflicting black youth did not consult any sociologists but did ask for insights from prominent economists. "As data from the Census Bureau suggests, while about 1.5 million Americans are economics majors, there is a far greater supply of psychology majors (3.4 million) and history majors (1.6 million), and only slightly fewer sociology majors (1.3 million)."[1]

As Chapter one of this book indicated, we are unlikely to advocate turning to historians for insights into reality nor are we going to kowtow to sociologists. "I can't get no respect," said Rodney Dangerfield and many professional sociologists may feel the same way but they have only themselves to blame.

The Ostrich

The ostrich, that head-in-the-sand symbol of denial, is an apt metaphor for humanity today. Being in denial of the reality that we sense is occurring around us is O.K. given that most of us can't cope any other way. Life is short and for many, religious beliefs encourage a focus on the afterlife as comforting compensation for our suffering. Religion-based narratives are also a way of keeping our focus on a story that offers a seemingly rational explanation for why things are the way they are. Nevertheless, there is a reason most of us are sand-eaters. Beware! Some of us may *not* want to know what that reason is.

Experiencing a different story that promises more immediate benefits than do religious paradigms and perhaps a more profound explanation for why our experience is what it is might persuade us to lift our heads and look around. It all boils down to making a choice of which narrative we choose to believe and in making that choice we become the creators of our identity and the experience which will then inevitably be the result of what we have chosen to believe. Worldview, identity and behavior; any profound scientific study of community (sociology) would be built around this structure.

The symbol of the ostrich represents a terrified and traumatized humanity that cannot bear to withdraw its head from the sand and look at what is happening. Those who try to face the facts are often overwhelmed. Who can blame them? With no criteria grounded in Simple Reality paralysis can occur when we are faced with choices that are agonizingly painful; choices based on delusional beliefs.

Which?
Which shall we choose?
    Should it be fear or compassion?
Which warrior shall we arm?
    The one who fights in a distant land OR
    The one seeking self-respect on a disputed street corner selling
        drugs?
    (They are the same warrior.)

Which wounds shall we bind?
> The shrapnel-incised bodies in the burning building of a foreign city OR
> The shattered psyches of our own self-medicated youth?
> (They are identical shattered souls.)

Which neighbor shall we comfort?
> The lonely aging man whose mind is slipping away OR
> The aging woman in the refugee camp, ankle deep in the mud.
> (They are the same lost and abandoned elders.)

Which rape victim shall we protect?
> The altar boy at St. Elizabeth's in Philadelphia OR
> The sari-clad teen in the slums of Mumbai?
> (They are our invisible and unprotected children.)

Which terrorist shall we execute?
> The bearded youth on the drone camera screen OR
> The tattooed Aryan White Supremacist in a Dallas prison?
> (They are the same deluded and angry seeker of respect.)

Which child shall we teach?
> The revenge-seeking child in the Middle Eastern madrassa OR
> The wealth-seeking child on Manhattan's Upper East Side?
> (They both suffer from the same self-destructive identity.)

Which mother shall we feed?
> The gaunt, starving Congolese mom cradling a dead baby OR
> The meth-craving Appalachian mom who cares nothing for food?
> (They both wander benumbed and lost in a nightmare.)

Which body shall we repair?
> The IED-shattered body lying by the roadside in Baghdad OR
> The bomb-shattered body on Boylston Street in Boston?
> (They are both innocent and bewildered.)

Which mind shall we rescue from the madness of a non-existent narrative?
> The bi-polar youth with empty eyes OR
> The dust-covered West Bank Palestinian hurling rocks?
> (They are the future; damaged by an identity they did not consciously choose.)

Obviously choices currently being made based on the conventional (P-B) beliefs, attitudes and values promulgated by the professional sociologist cannot result in a sustainable community. What is the fate awaiting the global village? It will be the four horsemen of the Apocalypse in spades. Worse than disease, famine, war and death? Afraid so!

Will the following description of dystopia paralyze you? Will you want to distract yourself and go shopping?

Add to the classic human woes, global warming and its effects and other natural calamities—tsunamis, hurricanes, tornadoes, floods, landslides, forest and grass fires, volcanic eruptions, drought, crop failures, extreme heat, extreme cold, earthquakes, antibiotic resistant superbugs and rising ocean levels inundating coastal environments. Given that 50% of the people in the global village live along continental coasts, the rising ocean levels seem to have caused widespread denial. Using a phrase from Garrison Keillor we will find that people are of "ordinary incompetence [but are also] a rigid and incurious people overwhelmed by events in a world they don't dare look around to see."[1]

What is wrong with this picture other than denying it is happening? Is there any way to change this gruesome looking future? First, we have to admit that there is a problem, which means facing reality. Economist Robert J. Samuelson explains why that hasn't happened yet. "We don't ask hard questions because we fear what the answers might be."[2]

You will be glad to know that there are two alternatives, two choices, but which is the best one? We will have to change our behaviors; that is obvious, but how? "The most powerful catalyst for change, sociologists will tell you, is when people learn what they already know."[3] The undeniable evidence coupled with our intuition (inner wisdom) is what we must base our future choices on.

If we don't choose to change our story we will continue to experience disturbing community metrics and behaviors. We are already seeing the following emerging dystopia.

Stress

"Colleges across the country are reporting an increase in the intensity of mental problems, including depression, stress and self-injury. In fact, the number of college counseling center clients on psychiatric medication rose from 9 percent to 25 percent in 2005, a University of Pittsburgh study said."[4]

Misogyny

"In a majority of the top-selling rap songs, women are cast as leeches deserving of mistreatment. They are used for sex, sometimes in [a] rough manner, then discarded. Some rappers even brag that they share their women with friends."[5]

Destruction of African American Families

"Black folks, by and large, don't do the marriage thing anymore. We are considerably less likely than white Americans (57% to 35%) to be currently married and similarly less likely (43% to 25%) to have ever been married. Largely as a result, 43% of our families are headed by single women, with all the problems of poverty and dysfunction that portends."[6]

Racism

"Although the deep problems afflicting poor black men have been known for decades, the new data paint the most alarming picture yet of ravaged lives and, the scholars say, of a deepening national calamity that has received too little attention. Terrible schools, absent parents, racism, the decline in blue-collar jobs and a subculture that glorifies swagger over work have all been cited as causes of the deepening ruin of black youths."[7]

Addiction

"I do not believe that gambling is harmless. As a criminal defense lawyer, I have witnessed the tremendous harm that gambling can bring about. I've watched the destruction of the addicted gambler, including one woman who was an otherwise blameless citizen until she began playing the slots. Casino managers watched as the machines ate first her salary, then her savings, and eventually the hundreds of thousands of dollars she embezzled from her employer. The casino bosses plied her with free rooms and dinners for her family. They sent a limo to bring her to the casino. They made her feel special as she fed huge quantities of $5 tokens into two machines simultaneously.

"They didn't come to court when she lost her dignity, her marriage, custody of her two children, and eventually her freedom. True, the state had no desire that she embezzle. But the state did repeatedly send the message that gambling was an approved activity."[8]

"Either we let Americans gamble legally or we don't. The growth of gambling outlets has indeed led to a rise in bankruptcy, suicide, robbery, embezzlement, divorce and other social ills. And state governments fool no one when they fund counseling organizations for people brought low by gambling activities that the states themselves raise revenues from."[9]

For those of us whose life has become a meditation by being in response to life moment by moment, by not resisting our life as it is, we find that our fear and suffering begins to diminish. As our skill in not allowing our old false-self conditioning to dictate our experience grows stronger, we learn how to use our energy to support the growing True-self conditioning resulting in a growing equanimity.

Living in the Now is too deeply satisfying, we wouldn't want to have our head in the sand and miss a single wonderful moment.

Crazy Metaphors? Maybe Not!

Zombies, vampires and sleepwalkers; the scarecrow, the tin man and the lion inhabit our psyches. They all make great metaphors for an unconscious and/or clueless humanity. But so do the hypnotized, the highly neurotic and the mentally ill. What about the psychopath and the sociopath, the unfeeling robot or Hal the malevolent computer? Are they just too "not human," too far out or too removed from our ability to relate to them for us to experience them as "like us."

One thing is for certain, whereas many of the metaphors we have used in enlivening our descriptions of Simple Reality were purely imaginary, many psychopaths walk among us unnoticed. That is because, you see, they are often highly intelligent and very clever at disguising their true emotions, or should we say lack of them.

The dictionary defines a psychopath as "a person with a personality disorder, especially one manifested in aggressively antisocial behavior." These are the psychopaths that exist in our imaginations because these are the ones portrayed in the headlines, books and movies. They stand out but, as we have just said, there are those that we don't see, that are clever at appearing normal and do not want to call attention to themselves.

Now let us return to the dictionary definition referring to "personality disorder" and "aggressively antisocial behavior." Since virtually all of us will become aggressive and antisocial when our survival is at risk, under the right conditions, we sometimes fit the definition of "antisocial." P-B is a worldview in which competition is valued over cooperation largely because the human condition is believed to be a dog-eat-dog struggle to claim a share of very limited assets, pleasures and power.

Our healthy True self when expressed would be compassionate and "non-grasping," given to sharing and to nurturing one another. We could say that this is normal or non-neurotic behavior. Because the True self personality is not the common experience of the bulk of humanity it is not a stretch to characterize much of humanity's day-to-day reactive behavior as "like" that of a psychopath if not strictly, clinically so.

So are we crazy? Of course! No sane person would willfully engage in self-destruction or choose and create suffering. Welcome to the Funny-Farm in America. We are not trying to increase your paranoia, we just need to "get real" about what is actually happening around us and what our identity and behaviors say about us. Failure to do this will only intensify our increasingly psychopathological behavior. Our descent into madness is something we don't want to know about but if we don't acknowledge it, we will have missed the opportunity for choosing to begin the ascent out of the darkness of our zombie-like, self-destructive behavior.

We should meet an actual sociopath to make our understanding of the actual identity and behavioral traits more vivid. M. E. Thomas' (a pseudonym) memoir, *Confessions of a Sociopath: A Life Hiding in Plain Sight*, supports the "bad news" aspect of the bleak future for a humanity mesmerized by the false self. Admittedly the vast majority of us suffer a different "kind" of sociopathy than does Thomas. Hers is severe. "Thomas self-identifies 'more as a sociopath than by my gender or profession or race.'"[1] She seems to have already gone over to the dark side while the rest of us are only headed that way.

Thomas considers herself a noncriminal sociopath but is perfectly capable of cruelty and total disregard for the feelings of others. Her lack of feeling ranges from letting a baby opossum drown in her swimming pool—"'I did not give it a thought'—to the time she cut off all ties to a friend whose father was dying of cancer because the woman wasn't fun to be around anymore."[2]

The Hare PCL checklist is used in psychopathy diagnosis. Among the descriptors are "glib" and "superficial" which explains why sociopaths are often less charming or interesting than they think they are. Pathological lying and lack of realistic long-term goals are two more identifiers to look for. No doubt, most of the behavioral traits of the human false self would be found in the clinically ill, probably just much more pronounced in the sociopath.

As a graduate student Daniel Kahneman was in a psychotherapy course where the professor warned about the charming, clever and manipulative psychopath. "'You will from time to time meet a patient who shares a disturbing tale of multiple mistakes in his previous treatment. He has been seen by several clinicians, and all failed him. The patient can lucidly describe how his therapist misunderstood him, but he has quickly perceived that you are different. You share the same feelings, are convinced that you understand him, and will be able to help.' At this point my teacher raised his voice as he said, 'Do not even *think* of taking on this patient! Throw him out of the office! He is most likely a psychopath and you will not be able to help him.'"[3]

The most alarming behavior in sociopaths, which is also becoming more prevalent in the global village population at large, is the lack of affect, the absence of "feeling" or compassion. This dying of the light of compassion as indicated by an increase in the ratio of reactions over responses in day-to-day life is a concrete measure of a society losing its grip on Simple Reality. The warning to take away from our exploration into sanity vs. insanity so far is to beware of the psychopath—beware of the false self—they are both capable of causing abject human suffering.

Perhaps zombies are not fictitious creatures at all. We could define a zombie (without including all of the gruesome Hollywood makeup and the awkward and sometimes comical shuffle) as being fearless, without emotions, and an inability to identify with and connect to other human beings. This is the way Thomas describes her behavior and indeed her memoir corroborates that this is her fundamental identity.

Thomas says that she believes she is a sociopath as a result of both nature and nurture. Scientists may one day find the sociopath gene imbedded in the human genome but if humanity would cease its denial, we can easily see how our environment, our story, is slowly isolating us from our fellow human beings and numbing our ability to feel compassion for one another.

If we were to place the True self and the false self on a continuum from maximum compassion (feeling) at one end and the "unfeeling" psychopath at the other we could see that most of us are not by a clinical definition "psychopaths." But without a healthy story and identity our dysfunctional behaviors are all too socio-pathological in their results.

For example, we can see some types of violence emerging that are difficult to explain or understand. Are all people behaving in an extremely anti-social way sociopaths? Take the suicide bomber. Few human behaviors could be more violent than mass murder while committing suicide. Clinically ill sociopaths are small in number but sociopaths produced by P-B are much more numerous than in the past and growing rapidly.

"A decade ago [2003] suicide bombings were still rare events. The political scientist Robert Pape counted a global total of 315 attacks from 1980, when they were first established as a modern terrorist method, through 2003. In the following two years, that number doubled. Today [2013], the total is more than two thousand, and each day seems to bring news of more."[4]

The suicide bomber is only one example of the growth of violence created by the self-alienation produced by our choosing illusion over Simple Reality. If we characterize the clinically ill sociopath as insane, we can also place that label on the terrorist who exhibits similar behaviors. However, from the perspective (narrative) of the suicide bomber, it is the U.S. that is the *other*, even as Americans are putting the same label on those who see themselves as defending their nation, culture or religion.

"In fiction [for example, John Updike's *Terrorist*] as in politics, the enemy's outlines grew vague and vast; he was too big to be tried in our courts, too deadly to be fought without torture, too radical to be understood. We imagined an enemy worthy of the grief and terror he causes us."[5] We "imagined" an enemy. There has never been a more profound human insight than these last words. We Americans have "imagined" the non-existent *other* just as anyone in the global village who contemplates violence "imagines" an enemy.

Simple Reality explains how ordinary young men and women who are otherwise mentally healthy, that is to say, not sociopaths, choose to turn themselves into human weapons. In the context of P-B, our sociologists and psychologists have not been able to explain these deeply disturbing and seemingly senseless acts of violence.

In Ziad Doueiri's film "The Attack" [2013], the wife of a successful Israeli-Arab surgeon blows herself up in a crowded Tel Aviv restaurant, killing 17 other people. This is a doubly disturbing suicide bombing because the bomber is atypical. The doctor tracks down the cleric who persuaded his wife to blow herself up and gets a typical P-B "non-answer." "If you haven't understood a thing since you set foot here, it means you probably never will."[6] Indeed, it is not possible to understand human behavior unless we can transcend the old story and the old identity which produces our self-destructive and deeply conditioned behaviors.

What we *can* come to understand is that both the clinically ill sociopath like Thomas and the Jihadi suicide bomber are in effect insane because suicidal or self-destructive behavior is madness no matter the cause or motivation. The human mind and the story that it tells itself have the power to entrap anyone in a cycle of self-destruction. Once entrapped in that maze, as the human condition demonstrates, the solutions of the ordinary human intellect are powerless to lead us to freedom.

Sam Byers, from the age of 17 to 32, despite trying many conventional solutions, could not overcome his addiction to smoking. Finally, he paid hypnotherapist Stella Knight $125 for a 20-minute session. "'People think you have to be stupid to be hypnotized,' she said, 'but actually it's actually the opposite. The best people to hypnotize are the most intelligent ones. You're going to be easy.'"[7]

When she brought him out of the trance, Stella was lighting up a cigarette. "'Why are you lighting a cigarette?' Byers asked. 'So you can say goodbye to it,' Stella said. What a load of bunk, I thought as I stood outside her bungalow. I had a packet of tobacco in my pocket (I had, of course, smoked heavily on the way over). I decided to take it out and think about having a cigarette, noting carefully my emotional response."

"The coughing fit that followed was both rapid and utterly debilitating in effect ... the fit lasted at least five excruciating minutes ... By the end I was exhausted and completely unable to imagine smoking for fear of triggering another bout of respiratory violence."

"In the weeks that followed, this happened again, always when I ordinarily would have smoked. I took these episodes for what they clearly were: welcome reminders of my boundless susceptibility to suggestion, which as any good hypnotist will tell you, is just another term for intelligence."[8] Most of us are hypnotized by our P-B identity. Each of us has the "wisdom within" to act as our own therapeutic hypnotist to free ourselves from our self-destructive habits.

As the human condition continues to express increasing violence, mental illness, and a general descent into chaos, we can choose to understand our role as individuals in this growing socio-pathology or we can choose to change our role and enlist the wisdom of the awakened mind in shifting our story and identity. We have boundless resources beyond the maze of P-B that will free us from the illusion of the *other* and the suffering created by our current socio-pathology.

We are crazy zombies all right even if we don't have the surface "appearance." The problem is not superficial. We will have to look deep within to escape from the Land of Oz.

He's Onto Something!

*Heads up! Look alive! Don't turn your back!
It's coming.*[1]

Readers of the Simple Reality books know that the zombie metaphor is often used to express the darker side of human behavior. Despite the fact that the zombie metaphor has been used in films since 1932 and along with the vampire metaphor in fiction well before that, most Americans probably don't grasp why the blank-faced shufflers fascinate us or what the deeper meaning of these metaphors is. One American, however, seems to come closer than most in understanding why we need to sound the alarm at the approaching hordes of the staggering undead.

We are referring to the author of *The Zombie Survival Guide* and *The World of Z,* Max Brooks. Max is the son of the writer/director Mel Brooks and the late actress Anne Bancroft. Billed as "the world's leading zombie expert" Brooks has been traveling around spreading the alarm about the coming of a kind of perfect storm represented by the metaphorical zombies.

"*W.W. Z.*" was featured on a reading list put together by a former president of the U.S. Naval War College, and Brooks has lectured at various army bases on zombie preparedness. He's a zombie laureate, our nation's lone zombie public intellectual, touring everywhere from Long Island to Ireland to Sugar Grove [Illinois] to prepare humans for the coming zombie plague."[2]

Like many of us, Brooks, realizing that we are not living on the planet in a sustainable way, experiences "high anxiety." If his neurotic hyper-vigilance is not occasioned by literal zombies, what is he afraid of? "'Since 2001, people have been scared,' he explained. 'There's been some really scary stuff that's been happening—9/11, Iraq, Afghanistan, Katrina, anthrax letters, D.C. sniper, global warming, global financial meltdown, bird flu, swine flu, SARS. I think people really feel like the system's breaking down.'"[3]

Indeed, the global village community is "breaking down" but that's hardly anything new. Fans of Simple Reality recognize Brooks' scary specters as symbols *of*, creations *of* and reactions *to* our own false self. We are literally scaring ourselves, that is to say that Max Brooks *is* a zombie. It does seem a little crazy that we would behave in a way that would cause anxiety for ourselves and others, but then, madness is an apt label for life in P-B.

"'Max could have been great at comedy,' says his father. 'He was going along those lines with S.N.L. [Max wrote sketches on Saturday Night Live for two years, 2001-2003], but his targets were bigger. His world is bigger than mine. The zombies aren't comedy. It has to do with life-and-death survival, the modus operandi for the need to survive. Not to be happy—that's something else. To survive.'"4

Max Brooks is indeed "onto something" but he hasn't quite figured out what that something is. He is only getting vague images, pulses from his self-created neurotic imagination. Brooks, the U.S. Naval War College and the U.S. Army are getting "freaked out" by the zombies contained in a story that exists only in their own minds, images emanating from a nightmare. They are trying to craft a *modus operandi* in reaction to "forms" they sense are "out there." The "something" out there is "no-thing." Nada. Phantasmagoria. Fighting the zombies, vampires and ghosts emanating from our own minds filled with fear will lead to chaos and destruction—our destruction.

Perhaps Brooks doesn't realize it but he is agonizing over the "theodicy question." Why do bad things happen to good people? Philosophers and intellectuals in the West have failed to give a satisfactory answer to this question without copping out and saying that only God can answer it. Siddhartha Guatama had more faith in humanity and articulated the response to the reality that "life is suffering." Max Brooks would do well to begin reading one of the several good books that translate the Buddhist *Suttas* and the *Dhammapada* into simple English. Dr. Walpola Rahula's *What the Buddha Taught* is an excellent book to start with.

And, of course, humanity's survival is exactly what the articles and essays found in the books of the Simple Reality project are about. What exactly threatens our survival and specifically what to do about it make Simple Reality a kind of "Perfect Storm Survival Guide" for the people of the global village. We could begin by ceasing to imagine that life consists of chasing and biting one another. What an utterly silly scenario for adults to create and derive their identities from.

Bad Choices

The history of the development of the unsustainable human community is not a chronicle of failure but rather a series of "bad choices." We begin this essay in what might seem to be a state of illogical confusion, but continue to hold on with the pedal to the metal—it will be worth your while—and worth burning a little rubber in your brain.

Once humanity chose P-B as its narrative, every human institution and every human endeavor was infected with false-self behaviors. The beliefs, attitudes and values among both individuals and collectives and what behavioral psychology calls "operant conditioning" rendered humanity unconscious.

The "bad choices" in question can still be rectified by both individuals and collectives including the global village but not in the way we might think. Those choices probably cannot be tweaked or modified or made better by becoming "good" boys and girls; in most cases they will have to be radically different choices—transcendent choices. Let's use for our example an old and venerated institution in the West, the Roman Catholic Church, and let it represent religion in general. Don't forget—we are presented with choices each and every day and it's never too late to change direction—but that direction must involve divergent thinking, something we are not used to doing.

Why do we need religion in the first place? As we start to answer that question we begin to see the rationale behind one of humanity's first "bad choices."

Those of us who subscribe to the principles of Simple Reality know that there is a deep psychological need to create a story in our craving for security. "A cosmos without known cause or fate is an intellectual prison; we long to believe that the great drama has a just author and a noble end."[1] Religion provides a foundation for a context that satisfies the human yearning for a "just author" or creator who is "fair" (even if in some religious myths, a tad judgmental) and also an end without anxiety—paradise.

By choosing P-B and the institution of religion that often comes with that choice, we have chosen an identity that leaves us powerless and forces us to engage in fear-driven and desperate delusional fantasies that the feverish human mind is adept at imagining. "The great majority of mankind feel compelled to ascribe mysterious entities or events to supernatural beings raised above 'natural laws.' Religion has been the worship of supernatural beings—their propitiation, solicitation, or adoration."[2] In this childish rejection of maturity humankind began the "soap opera" that has become our history, a melodramatic decline into a darkening paradigm of impotence and despair.

What about the growth of the human intellect or technological progress? Perhaps that will save us from our immature dependence on religion. "Science gives man ever greater powers but ever less significance; it improves his tools and neglects his purposes; it is silent on ultimate origins, values, and aims; it gives life and history no meaning or worth that is not cancelled by death or omnivorous time."[3]

Whatever we imagined the benefits of science or religion might be, the human false self has been in charge of what actually happened throughout our history. For example, the temptation of power would be only one influence corrupting the ideals of the Church. "The Church forgot the poverty of the Apostles in the needs and expenses of power ... Aeneas Sylvius, before becoming pope, wrote that everything was for sale in Rome."[4]

In choosing duality as our context, giving the false self a perfect playground, the fate of humanity was sealed. Despite attempts to reform the Church, the narrative that determined human identity had an overwhelming influence on human behavior. "The monasteries tried again and again to restore their austere rules, but the constitution of man [his false-self identity] rewrote all constitutions."[5] Even Buddhists driven by the twin motivators of craving (power) and aversion (fear) have recently resorted to self-destructive behavior in Myanmar (2013).

To book passage on a religious vessel will not take humanity where it wants and needs to go. All religious institutions are inherently leaky vessels. The Church, even after the Reformation, remained a flawed narrative that had every reason to keep the faithful in the dark where they were easier to fleece, deceive and abuse.

The youngest American religion is a case in point that all religions engage in lies, denial and secrets. Even though the "ship" of the Mormon Church is leaking like a sieve, it takes on about one million members every three years and currently (2013) has a worldwide membership of 13 million. Self-delusion is one behavioral trait that explains why when faced with a listing and sinking ship passengers pretend all is O.K. "I was just in a bubble and we felt so happy."[6]

The "happy" Hans Mattsson was an overseer for the Church of Jesus Christ of Latter-Day Saints throughout Europe. When logic can penetrate the smoke and mirrors that religion is so adept at manipulating, reality sometimes disturbs the rational mind. "But when he discovered credible evidence that the church's founder, Joseph Smith, was a polygamist, and that the Book of Mormon and other scriptures were rife with historical anomalies, Mr. Mattsson said he felt the foundation on which he had built his life begin to crumble."[7]

Remember denial? When someone suggests the ship has a hole in it and water is pouring in and believers think they are on the only vessel that can deliver them to paradise, they get very creative at rationalizing why their ship won't sink. Nevertheless, some find their way to the lifeboats and abandon ship. "A survey of more than 3,300 Mormon disbelievers, released in 2012, found that more than half of the men and four in ten of the women had served in leadership positions."[8]

Religion works best if the church communities are closed to influences from outside the community, that way doubt is more easily kept at bay, community secrets are more easily kept and the temptation to tell lies does not raise its ugly head as often.

Family relationships can be adversely affected by community members like the Mattssons who begin to ask awkward questions. When the Mattssons recently moved to Spain for health reasons, "They left behind some family members unhappy with Mr. Mattsson's decision to grant interviews to *The New York Times* and to the 'Mormon Stories' podcast."[9]

"I don't want to hurt the church," Mr. Mattsson said. "I just want the truth."[10] Unfortunately for Mr. Mattson and the rest of humanity searching for truth within a religious narrative, the truth is one of the first "passengers" tossed overboard along with healthy, sustainable beliefs, attitudes and values. Those who chose not to continue their voyage on the Mormon vessel and abandoned ship might have made a "good choice."

The insight that we live in a friendly universe would make a "good choice" not only possible but the option of "bad choices" would disappear. In the meantime, no Reformation or short-cuts, no changing vehicles or modes of travel, no reckoning by sophisticated technology or fervent prayer can keep our global vessel from sinking. One act alone, the "good choice" of distinguishing illusion from Reality will suffice.

The Implicate Order in the narrative of Simple Reality posits a creative process without end, beyond time and space, with heartfelt Perfection as the "always-at-hand experience" for those who find the courage to choose to awaken from P-B. Anxiety and "noble ends," craving and aversion, the pursuit of plenty, pleasure and power are poor justification for bad choices. The listing ship on which humanity sails will not be "righted" without the jettisoning of religion. All that canvas stored on our nuclear powered ship is an irrational clinging to past conditioning. We no longer need depend on the wind of illusion.

The Decline And Fall Of Practically Everybody

In the several books comprising the content of the Simple Reality Project we frequently find the claim that all is not well with the human community sometimes known as the global village, what we might call the "Human Empire."

Some would say that these claims are exaggerated and that over time humanity has evolved from barbarism to higher and higher states of civilization. Others claim that the veneer of civilization is rotten underneath and that human nature is fundamentally the same as it was in the ancient empires which all eventually imploded.

Some say that the progress created by comparatively recent advances in technology is evidence of the intellect's ability to find ways to lift humanity ever higher out of reach of apocalyptic poverty, disease, starvation and violence. Others say that only a small minority in the human community is benefiting from technology and that true progress is thwarted by the intellect which is incapable of addressing the increasingly intractable human condition.

Some say that the Creator never intended for the bulk of humanity to make progress on earth and will only find justified punishment in the afterlife where the smaller number of the well-behaved would be rewarded. Others claim that after countless reincarnations all of humanity will be able to progress in a complex system of reward and punishment and at last escape numberless rebirths in animal, vegetable or human form.

How can we measure the progress of the animal that reasons or that of his communities? Can progress or decline be detected? Is human behavior generally psychopathological? How prevalent are anti-social behaviors?

We all know, at least in our heart of hearts, that the prevalence of compassion in a community would be a good measure of its long-term success. How does it treat the "least" among its members? Maybe the following true story will offer some indication of whether humanity is facing good news or bad. Look for evidence of the aforementioned indicators of a healthy human community or one in decline. Don't forget to look for your own behaviors there too.

Like a pathologist we will slice out a cross section of the American Chinese/Korean immigrant community in Flushing, Queens. Photographer and amateur sociologist Yeong-Ung Yang is one of two "specialists" who will help us interpret the results revealed by this "tissue."

Like many cities in the U.S., casinos run buses from densely populated neighborhoods harvesting the spare change that rich or poor are willing to part with. Most of the Queens gamblers are bused to the Sands casino in Bethlehem, Pennsylvania. Yang has been documenting what he calls the "endless commute" of those who regularly ride these buses after they purchase a $15 ticket. As we shall see, many of these bus-kkun (bus riders in Korean) do not have $15 to spare.

Another Korean immigrant who arrived 14 years ago has been gambling at out-of-state casinos for years. Chun Hae-Young, age 57 reveals his own experience: "The casino is a kind of place that can bleed you dry of everything. It can also save your life when you have nothing."[1] How is such an irony explained?

If you can scrape together the $15 bus ticket you can become an admittedly strange entrepreneur. The casino offers free gambling and meal vouchers which you sell upon your return for a profit of around $40. Mr. Yang has observed that for these bus riders it's a job. "There are those that arrive at the casino and go straight to the waiting room and immediately start waiting for the next bus to go home."[2]

So there is the answer to our ironic behavior. The Sands casino can help reduce you to poverty if you become addicted to gambling but can also put food on the table especially if you are unable to work because of poor health or old age. Mr. Yang has looked hard at this issue from within his community in Queens and sees a double irony. "The whole routine itself, even though many are not gambling, is an addiction, and very hard to quit."[3]

The false self is vulnerable to addictive behaviors acquired while trying to survive physically but also while trying to escape physical and mental suffering. In a compassionate community, all of that energy could be used to reduce the very behaviors that threaten to cause the decline and fall of yet another empire.

Feeding Frenzy:
The Return Of The Stocks

Ignominy is universally acknowledged to be a worse punishment than death.
    Benjamin Rush
    (a signer of the Declaration of Independence)

Ignominy means being shamed, dishonored, humiliated or disgraced. This only happens when the "shaming" is public, that is to say, when others who know you or know about you witness your humiliation. A person living anonymously in a large city, for example, can commit shameful acts without suffering ignominy. Thanks to the worldwide web that kind of anonymity is often no longer available as a protection against the hostility of the inhabitants of the global village. The high-tech Big Brother nowadays is always watching.

Hordes of zombies—many of our fellow inhabitants in the global community—are engaging in a "feeding frenzy" of late; like bloodhounds frantically seeking the scent of anyone guilty of bad judgment. Jon Ronson coincidentally supports the metaphors we use in this essay in his article in *The New York Times Magazine* entitled "Feed Frenzy."

It's important that we get a good feel for the key word frenzy in this essay because it is, as we shall learn, an apt descriptor of the human condition. A frenzy is a temporary madness, manic activity, a violent agitation, wild excitement or delirium. Some brief historical examples of "feeding frenzies" and some occurring today will put the whole thing in perspective.

In colonial times public humiliation was used to punish transgressors of accepted moral behavior. The stocks, the pillory and the whipping post were commonly used in a public display that might make one wonder if the person "caught in the act" might have become a scapegoat for those who suffered their guilt in anonymity, those fortunate enough not to have been "caught in the act."

In 1742, Abigail Gilpin, whose husband was at sea *was* caught "'naked in bed with one John Russell.' They were both to be 'whipped at the public whipping post 20 stripes each.' Abigail appealed the ruling, but it wasn't the whipping itself she wished to avoid. She was begging the judge to let her be whipped early, before the town awoke. 'If your honor pleases,' she wrote, 'take some pity on me for my dear children who cannot help their unfortunate mother's failings.'"[1] Abigail feared the shame more than the lash.

The pillory, stocks and public whipping were abolished at the federal level in 1839 but not whipping in jails and prisons. An 1867 editorial in *The Times* pointed out why we should be concerned with the "return of the stocks" today. "If [the convicted person] had previously existing in his bosom a spark of self-respect, this exposure to public shame utterly extinguished it … The boy of 18 who is whipped at New Castle for larceny is in nine cases out of 10 ruined. With his self-respect destroyed and the taunt and sneer of public disgrace branded upon his forehead, he feels himself lost and abandoned by his fellows."[2] Not the result a truly compassionate community would be hoping for.

Before we turn to the form taken by public shaming today we have a couple more points to make about group behavior related to displays of violence in public. The first is denial. We don't like to admit how violent and cruel we can be and, secondly, we like to forget how we have behaved in the past. Many of us have seen old photographs of whites, including children, smiling and laughing at what might seem like a public picnic or holiday celebration until we notice in the background the dangling body of a lynched African American. Then we are shocked and sickened. Then we remember what we would prefer to forget. We remember that people are capable of ugly and cruel behavior in groups, much more so than as an individual.

As for the "forgetting" or denial of our history many of us are not aware that minorities other than African Americans were victims of extra-legal justice. From 1848 to 1928 mobs murdered thousands of Mexicans, though surviving records allowed us to clearly document only about 547 cases. These lynchings occurred not only in the southwestern states of Arizona, California, New

Mexico and Texas, but also in states far from the border, like Nebraska and Wyoming."[3]

Today, some perpetrators of violence are not ashamed following their acts of savage behavior and even want to display their gruesome acts of carnage so the whole world can suffer the shock of the unimaginable. Why? Has fear and paranoia driven some of us into advance states of psychopathology? Or maybe instead of extreme violence being a consequence of fear it is seen as a way to create fear. "Gavin Rees, the European director for the Dart Center for Journalism and Trauma, which focuses on the issues of reporting on violence helps explain: 'That is part of the gain for those who are producing these videos: They want to inspire fear and helplessness.'"[4]

We have perhaps reached new levels of violence on our planet and as Rees concludes, the terrorists are achieving their goal. "One of the things about traumatic imagery is that it can numb us and render us passive and helpless."[5]

If you think our imagery of violent zombies is an extreme metaphor for modern public violence, think again. "The Syrian government has made much of a video of an insurgent ripping the organs from a slain soldier and taking a bite."[6]

If the "return of the stocks" and public shaming and violence was the work of only political extremists or a regrettable but forgotten chapter of our historical past that might not be so bad, however the unfortunate truth is that the stocks are being deployed around the world today by millions of us.

What are the "stocks" in the 21st century, who gets put in them and who puts the victims there? Let's take Justine Sacco as an example of someone whose behavior offended her community. During the holidays in 2013, she was flying from New York to South Africa to visit her family and tweeted "Going to Africa. Hope I don't get AIDS. Just kidding. I'm White!" Justine had only 170 Twitter followers. By the time she landed in Cape Town after an 11-hour flight, her best friend Hannah tweeted "You're the No.1 worldwide trend on Twitter right now."

Sacco's intended meaning with her tweet was ambiguous but remember, people are always looking for scapegoats on whom to project their dissatisfaction with their life and who they are. Sacco had quickly become for thousands of people in less than half a day that scapegoat. She was quickly put in the stocks. "By the time her plane had touched down, tens of thousands of angry tweets had been sent in response to her joke."[7]

Jon Ronson offers his personal insight into why so many people show up in the public square to witness and use sites like Twitter to take part in 21st century lynchings. "Still, in those early days, the collective fury felt righteous, powerful and effective. It felt as if hierarchies were being dismantled, as if justice were being democratized. As time passed, though, I watched these shame campaigns multiply, to the point that they targeted not just powerful institutions and public figures but really anyone perceived to have done something offensive. I also began to marvel at the disconnect between the severity of the crime and the gleeful savagery of the punishment. It almost felt as if shamings were now happening for their own sake, as if they were following a script."[8] That script is called P-B.

Back to Justine Sacco whose experience in the stocks tends to be all too typical and all too sad. The punishment tends to be severe and lengthy. Modern Americans seem to be more vengeful than our colonial ancestors. Those who gather on social media to jeer at the person being shamed are not content with public shaming (which occurs on a worldwide scale) but they put pressure on employers to fire the hapless victim, and they usually do. The shaming can go on for months and months, the zombies are relentless and insatiable until they tire and move on to the next victim. Sacco lost her job and had to go into hiding eventually before she found new employment and escaped the stocks.

Why do people like Sacco bring these attacks upon themselves? The answer is found in the affection/esteem energy center of the false-self survival strategy. "Her tormentors were instantly congratulated as they took Sacco down, bit by bit, and so they continue to do so. Their motivation was much the same as Sacco's own—a bid for the attention of strangers [remember

Anthony Wiener]—as she milled about Heathrow, hoping to amuse people she couldn't see."[9]

Sometimes it's hard to tell whether we are witnessing compassion or fear-driven projection on the Internet. For example, women can use shaming or create a feeding frenzy by banding together to defend themselves against sexual harassment. "'From the plaintiff's perspective, it's one of the great equalizers, allowing women to gain ground against well-funded defendants,' said Debra Katz, a Washington lawyer who has been bringing employment and sexual harassment suits for three decades."[10]

Our colonial ancestors were very afraid of the wilderness, the Indians and unconsciously of chaos. Public shaming and witch-burning were expressions of this fear and represented their attempts to maintain control of their tenuous grasp on civilization. Is our legal system about to spin off into an Internet-centered chaos and what sort of paranoid psychopathology will accompany it?

"Leigh Goodmark, another Maryland law professor, said the online boom of gender-related court documents was a harbinger of a future in which virtually no legal document—an eviction notice, a divorce pleading with embarrassing details—would be safe from public consumption. 'Things people never bargained on getting out will get out,' she said."[11]

You have perhaps heard the Cherokee Indian folk tale of the young maiden who related a reoccurring dream that she was having to a tribal elder. She told of a white wolf and a black wolf fighting in her nightmarish dream and asked the elder who would win. He replied, "The one you feed."

The black wolf, the bloodhound and zombies are all metaphors for the false self. The false self salivates at the thought of pursuing plenty, pleasure and/or power. But the false self is also very, very afraid. This makes the fearful person very, very dangerous.

Our false self's need for *others* onto which to project its discontent has us using our social media to become both the one who shames and the shamed, the shooter and the target. Until we come to admit and understand how we choose to feed the black wolf, we will never experience the peace afforded by anonymity or the silence, solitude and simplicity we experience by feeding the white wolf. Given that the Internet is the most vital engine of our culture today we need to decide which wolf we want to feed.

Discouraging Compassion

This essay was started on October 5, 2014 and the subject was ostensibly driving cars while using cell phones and the tragedies that can result when combining these two activities. We talk a lot these days about this problem and many others with numerous insights into what to do about these many threatening and often self-destructive behaviors—but nothing happens—our behaviors remain the same. What is this paralysis in the face of irrational behavior? Are we cruel or crazy?

We now begin the process of broadening our inquiry by looking at what has come to be called "attention science." Studying the intersection of technology and human behavior, also called cognitive neuroscience which began in World War II with helping pilots and radio operators from being overwhelmed by the new technology they were learning to use. Not surprisingly, operators of the devices learned what we are also aware of today, namely, pay strict attention to what you are doing, that is to say, *be present.*

The problem with paying attention is that we don't want to. We invest a lot of energy in purposely distracting ourselves. Why? Well, because this is our chief strategy for avoiding suffering or in denying that our lives are dissatisfying. If we are not aware of what is really happening we can perhaps create an illusionary (made-up) story and convince ourselves that the identity determined by that story is really us, that our "new" *we* and our resulting "new" life is O.K.

Robert Kolker reviewing Matt Richtel's book on how and why we distract ourselves and the consequences of doing so agrees that Americans work hard to stay unconscious. "We are distracted because we want to be. Why else would they sell so many smartphones? As Richtel explains, a good gadget is essentially magical, commandeering our focus with delight and surprise and ease (Steve Jobs used the word "magical" about the iPhone when it debuted)."[1]

In September 2006, young Reggie Shaw, distracted while talking on his cell phone with his girlfriend, crashed into a car killing James Furfaro and Keith O'Dell. Shaw's story later became part of a 35-minute AT@T public service announcement directed by Werner Herzog released in 2013. The message of the film "From One Second to the Next" is part of AT@T's campaign against texting and driving.

Matt Richtel won a Pulitzer Prize for a series of articles he wrote about distracted driving in *The New York Times*. This year (2014) Richtel's book *A Deadly Warning: A Tale of Tragedy and Redemption in the Age of Attention*, includes Shaw's story of "redemption."

If Americans were immersed in the context of Simple Reality, our True selves would respond to the facts surrounding texting while driving and we would simply not use our cell phones while driving. That would be a compassionate response. But we live in P-B which effectively discourages compassion. In fact, the story that we tell ourselves encourages Americans to conceal, lie about and deny the truth. Instead of considering the suffering of our fellow human beings, a True-self response, our false-self hunkers down in a reaction of fear and self-preservation.

A community, wherein genuine compassion is discouraged and self-promotion and self-protection are paramount behaviors, will not long survive or at least will not be fit for human habitation. We return to the tragic events in the life of Reggie Shaw. "A fundamentally decent teenager, Shaw nevertheless had things he was ashamed of and family expectations to live up to. His pattern, even before the crash, was to dissemble [to disguise or conceal behind a false appearance—a decidedly false-self behavior] in order not to make trouble for those around him. Once the tragedy happened, Richtel writes, 'the intensity with which the family undertook the defense had a self-perpetuating and escalating force: Reggie denied texting, the family backed him up and Reggie, never someone to let others down, dug deeper.'" [2]

Our false-self identities determined by the P-B narrative create behaviors that escalate and intensify our suffering and so it was with Reggie Shaw. Compassion was nowhere in sight. "Should Reggie be charged with negligence or manslaughter, or nothing at all? Even if texting and driving is wrong, should he have known that? In Richtel's sensitive account, we come face to face with the horrible Catch-22 of accident litigation that discourages one party from apologizing to another, for fear of admitting liability [enter the lawyers, exit compassion]. This apparent standoffishness helped persuade the prosecutor to make Shaw a test case for texting and driving. Which in turn caused Shaw's family to accuse the prosecutor of waging a witch hunt. Which only appalled the victim's widows and families and advocates even more."[3]

Shaw began to travel the country making speeches, a spokesman for those behaviors that flow naturally from compassion, speaking out against those which cannot be countenanced if they cause danger and pain to others. He found a way to stop reacting; he learned the deeply meaningful joy of responding in the context of Simple Reality.

But what about the rest of us? Are we finding the courage to look at our dysfunctional behaviors? Why do we persist in driving while texting, for example? "Richtel tries out several analogies to describe the rush we get from a phone: alcohol, drugs, television, video games, junk food, the fight-or-flight response [reaction] to a tap on the shoulder … Our bodies love the little hit of dopamine we get each time we check our phones for something, anything."[4]

Yes, our false self loves each little hit of dopamine. And we must find the courage to look at our dysfunctions, one by one, and choose compassion.

Euphoria Or Dysphoria: Virtual Delusion

The term "virtual reality" coined in the 1980s usually has meant the use of a headset to achieve an immersive and realistic audio-visual illusion. Both NASA and the military have used the virtual reality technology to create flight and combat simulations. Unfortunately, both the government and commercial applications have been troubled by simulation or "sim" sickness.

So far developers have not overcome the motion sickness problem nor the very high cost of trying to get an acceptable product to market. "Recreational virtual reality flamed out in the 1990s with a handful of unfun, overhyped and physically sickening arcade games by a company called Virtuality. Developers like eMagin, Vuzix and Nintendo still quietly plugged along, but the persistent nausea problem turned V.R. development into a grim, frustrating, even embarrassing business."[1] Until today, that is, and now we have what might sound like an over hyped breakthrough called the Oculus Rift

"Indeed, fans of the Oculus Rift discover a pleasure so deep that John Carmack, Oculus's chief technology officer, invokes it with a particular solemnity. It's called 'presence.' To achieve presence with an Oculus headset means to be suffused with the conviction—a cellular conviction, both unimpeachable and too deep for words—that you are in another world."[2] Before we get too excited, those of us who are more conversant with the concepts of "reality" can recognize the language of Madison Avenue. But let's continue; there is much we can learn from this search for "presence" because, after all, that's what the Simple Reality Project is all about.

The word simulacrum often appears in the discussion of virtual reality. Among the many definitions of that word the one most applicable for our purposes in this essay is "an unsatisfactory imitation or substitute." Wow! The human condition can involve more than a little desperate distraction with endless pseudo-pleasures. Thoreaus' "Most men go to the grave living lives of quiet desperation with their song still in them" is apropos in explaining our current relationship with many of our high-tech "devices."

What if the experience of simulated reality as described above by John Carmack has the effect of "feeling" like we are "singing our song"? Norman Chan explained on tested.com that a virtual world does not feel like the old P-B reality. "But with presence ... you do get a profound sensation of space, causing you to forget you're staring at a screen. Presence is fragile, but when achieved, it's so joyful and sustaining that those who touch it tend to fall silent."[3]

If this reminds us of Timothy Leary's and Stan Grof's research with LSD or the effects of certain types of mushrooms or DMT, a powerful psychedelic compound, then we are well-advised to be skeptical. Virginia Heffernan, reporting on the virtual-reality phenomenon, asked one of the developers of V.R. about the relationship between hallucinogens and V.R. produced "presence." "'Oh I like Oculus *and* drugs' one virtual-reality curator told me, as if in reassurance. Maybe I shouldn't have been surprised. This is a crowd that likes to hallucinate."[4] Alas, this "crowd" that likes to hallucinate is some 7 billion self-medicating souls on this planet.

The conflict inherent in differentiating P-A from P-B may be showing up in the human body as it entertains the escape into V.R. "Under the spell of V.R., the eyes and ears tell the brain one story, while deeper systems—including the endocrine system, which registers stress; the vestibular, which governs balance; and other proprioceptors, which make spatial sense of the body's position and exertions—contradict it. The sensory cacophony is so uncanny and extraterrestrial to suggest to the organism a deadly threat."[5] This is, of course, precisely why identification with the body must be transcended.

"If nausea is the body's dysphoric response to the uncanny, presence is the euphoric one."[6] When John Carmack uses "feeling" and Virginia Heffernan in the previous sentence uses "presence" in describing sensations associated with the experience of V.R. they have not achieved the "feeling" of the "present moment" experienced by those in P-A.[g] In fact, our pursuit of V.R. sensations betrays our desperation to escape the illusion of our suffering; we seek a *future* illusion in trying to escape the *current* illusion (P-B).

It is fitting that the phrase "virtual reality" first makes its appearance in a play "The Theater and Its Double" (1938) by Antonin Artaud who sought to make his audience feel powerless and paranoid as he engulfed them in his "theater of cruelty." We can see that P-B has the same effect on the people of the global village today as most of us play our roles in what may be termed the "theater of the absurd."

It is ironic that the heart of distinguishing illusion from reality also requires experiencing the difference between response and reaction. Let me digress for a moment and break that down into defined chunks.

- Illusion – the fundamental cause of human suffering
- Reality – the insights that will emancipate humanity from all of its problems
- Response – presence or feeling, present moment
- Reaction – resistance or fear of our experience

Developers of V.R. reveal their ignorance of this distinction in their descriptions of the sensations of Oculus Rift. "In our gentler commercial idiom, used for movies and games, in which escape from reality is considered a *given good*, this comfort is known magisterially as *presence*."[7] (Italics added for emphasis.) Humanity has for many millennia become almost infinitely creative in escaping reality but few of us would believe that this has resulted in a "given good."

Expanding the context of this V.R. technology to include the human condition we see an analogy that has a global population searching for the vivid experience of the present moment but

---

[g] More about Feeling vs Emotion and Present Moment can be found in *Simple Reality* published books and on the blog http://mysimplereality.com

instead choosing the nauseating experience of the P-B delusion. We all long for what seems to be desirable and for exciting sensations that promise to intensify our experience of something pleasurable but lead us inevitably to the conclusion many Buddhists came to long ago, namely that many things cause suffering, including pleasure. (Which is a good "lead-in" to our next essay.)

Happiness Is Pursuit Of Security, Sensation And Power—Not!

Circumstances don't seem to have much effect on happiness.
           Daniel Kahneman

As the previous essay more than hinted at, most of humanity behaves as if they live in a delusional virtual reality, a reality that is imagined; a reality that is a product of a panic-stricken false self. Not only are our various communication and entertainment "devices," which are products of an impressive technologically sophisticated intelligence, not relieving our stress in the 21st century, they are contributing to our nausea and neuroses. Simply put, and more broadly conceived, the energy centers security, sensation and power of the false-self survival strategy, leading to the ever-more frantic pursuit of plenty, pleasure and power, are only intensifying human suffering.[h] Let's take a look at why this is so.

Are we being a bit melodramatic in our somewhat gloom and doom prognostication about the failure of community in America? We will put forth our facts and opinions along with other analysts and reporters and you be the judge. "In 2002 the World Mental Survey found that Americans were the most anxious people in the 14 countries studied, with more clinically significant levels of anxiety than people in Nigeria, Lebanon and Ukraine."[1] And that is just for starters!

Throughout human history, in the West at any rate, happiness has loomed large as a measure of success in a given community. Aristotle thought that happiness in ancient Greece consisted of being a moral or virtuous person. Followers of

---

[h] More about the energy centers security, sensation and power of the false-self survival strategy can be found in *Simple Reality* published books and on the blog http://mysimplereality.com

Epicurus felt that a good life would consist of the pursuit of pleasure within reasonable limits, of course. Along came the Christians and the regulation of those pleasures became much more severe. In fact, Christians felt that pleasure should be avoided altogether "and regarded pain as the more useful path to, if not a happy life, then a sort of divine union in the afterlife. That desired state could not be attained in life on earth, but only as a gift from God, in heaven."[2] Nothing profound so far, let's continue with the evolution of Western thought *vis-à-vis* happiness.

The Renaissance saw the search for happiness return to earth, a much more realistic and fruitful place to continue our search for human happiness. It was in the American colonies during the Enlightenment that happiness was conceived of as a political "right." This unalienable right was tied in with property and the emergence of what was once known as the Protestant Ethic but is understood in the context of Simple Reality as a more universal expression of the false-self pursuit of plenty, pleasure and power. Americans have long valued having, doing and knowing and it is not proving to be a source of happiness.

"And unlike the work-shy Greeks of antiquity [and perhaps today as well], we are assumed to find happiness through work and by being productive. We are required to curate our market value, manage ourselves as corporations and live according to an entrepreneurial ethos. When no sin is greater than being unemployed and no vice more despised than laziness, happiness comes only to those who work hard, have the right attitude and struggle for self-improvement."[3] Ah hah! But which self, there are two you know. But perhaps we don't know that. In which case, no wonder we are having trouble. Oh well, onward and uhhh—not upward—unfortunately because we are headed for that other place.

Security and Materialism

Our myriad strategies for escapism and self-medication are as old as humanity itself and have only gotten more complex and obsessive over time. Do they work? Do they assuage our fears? Do they relieve our stress? Do they increase our happiness? Unfortunately no!

The virtual reality or what *seems* to be true is that Americans are better off today than in the past in terms of prosperity. "If you made a graph of American life since the end of World War II, every line concerning money and the things that money can buy would soar upward, a statistical monument to materialism. Inflation-adjusted income per American has almost tripled. The size of the typical house has more than doubled."[4]

Measuring happiness then in America in roughly the last half century one would expect that, given a more prosperous population, we would be a happier community. "In polls taken by the National Opinion Research Center in the 1950s, about one-third of Americans described themselves as 'very happy.' The center has conducted essentially the same poll periodically since then, and the percentage remains almost exactly the same today [2005]."[5] We need to take a closer look at the connection between happiness and prosperity or more accurately, security and materialism.

It is not that money and happiness are not related but rather that income as a source of happiness has its limitations. The median annual income of a U.S. household in 2005, the year that *TIME* magazine took its poll, was $43,000. "*TIME*'s poll found that happiness tended to increase as income rose to $50,000 a year. After that, more income did not have a dramatic effect."[6]

Why are so many of us not able to find greater happiness and security with greater prosperity? It seems to be that our focus is not on our improved circumstances but rather on how well our neighbors are doing relative to our success. This keeping-up-with-the-Joneses phenomenon sociologists call "reference anxiety."

Edward Diener, a University of Illinois psychologist, interviewed members of the *Forbes 400*, the richest Americans who should be happy if money is a measure of happiness, right? Diener, however, found those with great wealth only slightly happier than Americans as a whole. "Because those with wealth often continue to feel jealousy about the possessions or prestige of other wealthy people, even large sums of money may fail to confer well-being."[7] Well, too bad, it looks like money is not going to be able to relieve our existential suffering and turn it into happiness.

Sensation and Escape

Sometimes when would-be sociologists are examining human behavior they may think that the goal of those behaviors is material wealth (money). What people are actually seeking is an escape from anxiety and/or ennui. They want the "experience" of say gambling, the "process" of playing poker or pulling the lever (now its pushing a button) on the "one-armed bandit." Winning any money at these games is incidental to the self-deception that leads to process addiction, as opposed to substance addiction.

You might think that seeking material wealth (money) emanates from the security energy center of the false self. But instead our behaviors place us firmly in the arena of the sensation energy center of the false self which is running full tilt away from terrors most of us can only imagine. In fact, we only "sense" our demons since they are for the most part unconscious or imagined. What we need to realize is that we are all engaged in similar delusions and in this general way we are all perpetuating a world with more suffering.

What does this look like specifically? Americans must be having more and more trouble with boredom and fear of late because gambling is a burgeoning industry. Let's pay a brief visit to the "sports book," a large two-story room with 31 cinema-scale screens in the Las Vegas Hotel & Casino showing myriad races and games. "Dogs and horses sprinted around tracks, men and women ran up and down basketball courts, football players launched themselves into one another."[8]

To be sure, money was being made by the insiders in the room and elsewhere, but not by the masses all across the U.S. and abroad betting on every imaginable contest and game epitomized by the noise, glamour and intoxication present in this room. Take a shallow, excited breath and go numb (that's what it's all about in gambling resorts) and pretend that this senseless, mind-numbing activity is providing happiness and excitement.

More and more American lemmings are running as fast as their little legs will carry them hell-bent on hurling themselves off the "Cliffs of Dover," a self-destructive, insane behavior by any definition. "One in five American men polled by researchers at

Fairleigh Dickinson University (and nearly one in 10 women) said that they bet on sports in 2012. In Nevada, where it is legal to bet via licensed bookmakers, the industry collected $3.4 billion in wages in 2012, nearly twice as much as a decade ago."[9]

One way to measure the increasing fear in America is to look at the proliferation of casinos. "'In the Northeast and mid-Atlantic states,' a report from the Institute for American Values notes this year, 'nearly every adult now lives within a short drive of a casino.'"[10] Whether it's Americans seeking escape and distraction from anxiety and boredom or capitalists and politicians seeking plenty and power, the gambling industry can expect ample support. "The spread of casinos has been more of a top-down phenomenon driven by states seeking revenue and an industry that's free with campaign contributions."[11]

The most dysfunctional communities in the global village tend to victimize women, children and the elderly disproportionally. The American community exhibits this callousness. "Women and the elderly have become more likely to gamble in recent years, partly because of a preference for nonskill slot-machine gambling."[12]

Simple Reality relies on profound insights into the psychology of human behavior. So does the gambling industry. A person addicted to gambling can bet as little as a penny on the "slots." Why does a casino bother with such small fry? Don't be puzzled. The casinos know how to cater to their victims' neurotic yearnings. Dollars are just a lot of pennies. "Most regional casinos are essentially slot parlors. Slot machines are nowadays sophisticated computerized devices engineered to produce continuous and repeat betting and programmed by high-tech experts to encourage gamblers to make multiple bets simultaneously by tapping buttons on the console as fast as their fingers can fly."[13]

We've already noted that the goal of the gambler is not to win but to enter into a mesmerized state that blocks out their existential suffering. Natashsa Dow Schull, an anthropologist at MIT who studied the design of gambling machines noted that "as gamblers deepen their immersion, they become less interested in winning itself than in simply continuing to play."[14]

Now we penetrate more deeply into the diseased mind of the gambler. Unlike hand-grenades and horseshoes, a near miss in a slot machine is rewarding. "One way these computerized pickpockets milk their customers is by generating 'near misses,' whereby the spinning symbols on the machine stop just above or below the winning payline. The feeling of having come oh so close to a win prompts further play."[15]

Since it is the American false self that drives our behavior, we know it behooves us to look for the dark side of all self-medicating behaviors. "Casinos tend to lower property values and weaken social capital [undermining long-term social welfare] in the places where they're planted, they're more likely to extract dollars from distressed communities than to spur economic development, and their presence is a disaster for the reckless and the addiction-prone."[16]

We know this so why are they still there?

Transitioning from process addictions to substance addictions we find even conservatives like Milton Friedman questioning our policy-makers who fail to understand the conditioned behaviors of those who identify with the false self. "Friedman became a hero to many good citizens who did not care to stand between a drug addict and his fix. To Friedman, the war on drugs was not a moral crusade. It was just plain stupid."[17]

Both process addictions and substance addictions (which more and more Americans are willing to legalize) are reflected in changing attitudes toward marijuana. Not only are more of us willing to accept pot as harmless or beneficial but also as a tempting source of much needed revenue. "The permissive turn on marijuana has been a more (if you will) grass-roots affair—driven by activists and artists, influenced by empathy for the terminally ill, and hastened by public exhaustion with the drug war."[18]

Failure to understand why we behave the way we do has the American community bewildered as our institutions continue to descend into chaos. With local and state governments lacking needed revenue, politicians willing to do and say anything to win votes and the private sector seeking to please shareholders, a P-B coalition has emerged to profit from a universal human weakness.

Common sense and Simple Reality could go hand-in-hand in crafting a response to substance abuse that would be more effective than current policies which are indeed stupid because they cause problems rather than solve them. Friedman wrote a letter to Bill Bennett, the drug czar under George H.W. Bush revealing a more profound understanding of false-self behavior than prevailed in that administration. "Your mistake is failing to recognize that the very measures you favor are a major source of the evils you deplore … Illegality creates obscene profits that finance the murderous tactics of the drug lords; illegality leads to the corruption of law enforcement officials; illegality monopolizes the efforts of honest law forces so that they are starved for resources to fight the simpler crimes of robbery, theft and assault."[19]

At one time Friedman was a member of the Marijuana Policy Project. They wanted to make marijuana a regulated and legal product like tobacco and alcohol. "One study suggests that ending the U.S. prohibition against marijuana could produce savings of nearly $8 billion a year and generate over $6 billion in tax revenues. Friedman and about 500 other leading economists endorsed the findings."[20]

Froma Harrop, intuiting the obvious, argued in her column in 2006 for legalization of drugs which only now in 2015 has begun with marijuana. "Put the drug dealers and narco-terrorists out of business by providing free drugs to our addicted populations. That way, we know who the abusers are and can offer them treatment. And those who persist in their addictions wouldn't have to prey on the rest of us for their drug money."[21] Harrop was robbed at knifepoint of a flute she was carrying on the subway, from someone who might have been desperate for the $40 a used and battered flute could be fenced for.

We close this arena describing how the false self seeks pleasure (sensation, affection and esteem) with one last major problematic behavior colloquially known as the munchies. Ha! Ha! Ha!—but wait—there is nothing funny about this addiction or this obsessive compulsive disorder (OCD). The annual global cost of obesity ($2 trillion) is almost equal to smoking or to armed violence, war, and terrorism combined. By 2030 The McKinsey Global Institute predicts that almost half of the world's adult population will be overweight or obese. That's up from the current 30 percent.[22]

The facts above are not what interests most people because most of us already know compulsive eating is a problem. Many of us use food to help us feel better. However, what we should have the courage to admit is first, that we must be suffering a lot to use food in this way; secondly, it doesn't work; and finally, it's getting worse. Is this what we want? We obviously think it is because many of us choose it—but probably not consciously. What other destructive conscious and unconscious behaviors darken our future?

Power and Happiness

The three energy centers of the false self can overlap and a single unconscious activity can involve the pursuit of plenty, pleasure and power simultaneously. More bang for the buck as it were. The process of betting on sports can bring a delusional escape from suffering but so can attending sports contests and experiencing a vicarious sense of power especially if our team is the winner and more-so if our team is a *big* winner. "It was the clear crushing of an opponent that most elicited this tendency to wear clothing that announced your association with the team. It's about power and superiority."[23] This is one way to create a sense of community but it is not going to be a sustainable community, not a healthy community.

Remembering the American cities used as symbols of each of the illusions[i] we use to deny reality, New York the seat of Wall Street (plenty) and Las Vegas (pleasure), we conclude this essay with a brief look at Washington D.C. (power).

---

[i] More about the American cities used as symbols can be found in *Simple Reality* published books and on the blog http://mysimplereality.com

Although many Americans persist in their beliefs that material wealth can bring them security and that pleasurable sensations can ease their suffering, they don't appear to have faith that their representatives in Washington can be counted on to provide the leadership to create a sustainable community. Not that the Washington-based military-industrial-corporate complex is without power, it's just that said power is not being used on the behalf of ordinary Americans.

Democratic strategist Doug Sosnik published this assessment in *Politico*. "He cited a Gallup poll in late June [2012] that showed that Americans' faith in each of the three branches had dropped to what he called 'near record lows,' with only 30 percent expressing confidence in the Supreme Court, 29 percent in the presidency and 7 percent in Congress."[24]

However, even with that pitifully low poll rating of 7 percent, in 2012, 90 percent of the House members and 91 percent of the senators who ran for re-election won. They must have some power somewhere. But in truth, there is no authentic power in Washington or anywhere else in P-B; but that is the subject for another essay.

Many of the essays in the Simple Reality Project advocate the expression of compassion as the most satisfying behavior for an individual and the most effective way for a community to achieve sustainability. In the U.S. today, most Americans are supporting exactly the opposite behaviors. No compassionate society would allow the existence of payday lending businesses, rent-to-own stores, subprime credit cards, auto title loans and loans based on anticipated tax refunds. All of these extract unconscionably high profits from defenseless vulnerable low income groups.

Having the most powerful military in the world, a gun in every closet, taking drugs to self-medicate, using gambling as a distraction and a community-wide denial of reality, no matter how assiduously all these behaviors are pursued, they only provide the illusion of safety, power, prosperity and happiness; when in fact we are engaged in self-destruction.

We have taken only a brief glance at human behavior but have seen enough to conclude that Americans and by inference, the rest of the world which follows our lead, however reluctantly, are becoming less healthy and more dysfunctional. Given that we could be making radically different choices in creating our community, this is indeed a sad state of affairs.

War Weary?

The Nature of the Universe

*Kind Lady Venus, cause the savage work of war
to rest in calm surcease throughout the sea and land.
For you, and you alone, can bless mankind with quiet
peace; all the savage work of war is ruled by Mars
the warrior, who often sinks upon your breast
a helpless victim of the quenchless wound of love;
with supple neck supine, he gazes up to you,
feasting his greedy eyes and drinking in your beauty,
a captive hanging helpless on your breathing lips.
Embrace him with your sacred body, Lady Venus,
and while he lies enraptured, speak sweet pleading words
beseeching him to grant the Romans rest and peace.*
     Lucretius

The Roman poet Lucretius seems to believe that reason and logic can solve all of humankind's problems including our propensity to seek solutions through the activity of warfare. Mystics understand that a deeper realization will be necessary for peace on earth.

One human behavior common between and within nations today is the waging of war. History tells us it has always been thus. Our tolerance for mass violence seems to be inexhaustible and it's been said that every day of every year there is a war being fought somewhere in the global village. "If the last 500 years have shown us anything, it is that radical change happens, repeatedly. Yet in their[j] cheery tour of the last few centuries, they never grapple with a still troubling truth: The evolution of the 'ever-improving' Western system of governance is inextricably bound up with mass carnage."[1]

---

[j] The authors of *The Fourth Revolution: The Global Race to Reinvent the State*.

In a quick review of western civilization, although the facts are well known to students of history, they bear repeating. "The modern nation-state emerged out of the religious wars that decimated Central Europe in the 17th century, while the 18th and 19th century reforms praised by the authors[k] were bound up with the American and French Revolution, the Napoleonic wars, the Franco-Prussian War and the wars of Italian unification, among others. Adjusting for population size, the death rates in these conflicts were staggering—and this is to say nothing of the wars of colonial domination that helped fuel the West's economic expansion. The emergence of the modern welfare state is similarly bound up with the 20th century's two catastrophic wars."[2] And we have entered the 21st century not knowing what the future will bring—except for those of us who are familiar with the false self—we know that war will be our constant companion.[3]

In other words the "progress" of Western civilization includes war without end. Why? Perhaps when we tire of war we will begin to seriously question why we would support such egregiously disastrous behavior. Perhaps you, dear reader, would like to form a group interested in taking action against the madness of collective violence—yes, an anti-war movement. But surely, you realize that such movements in the past have been abject failures, so clearly you will have to do something different. You will need to have a more profound understanding of this particularly pernicious human behavior. To that end we offer this analytical essay.

Before we begin to analyze the problem of war we will offer a solution on how to avoid war in the future, starting with a note of hope before we sound the ominous chord of civilization's demise.

Any and all behaviors to avoid widespread violence among nations, tribes, sects, religious or political factions, must begin with the insight that the existence of the *other* is an illusion. If Oneness is not the guiding principle upon which the quest for peace is founded, which would negate any belief in *other*-ness, then perpetual war on the planet is unavoidable. The following example

---

[k] The authors of *The Fourth Revolution: The Global Race to Reinvent the State*.

makes clear that without acceptance and compassion we cannot live side-by-side with our neighbors without minor differences escalating into mass slaughter. The illusion of the *other* grows stronger day by day in the Middle East and in particular in Israel where Israelis and Palestinians can't seem to find the room wherein a successful peace can be negotiated. The doorway to that room is blocked by a growing belief in the existence of the *other*. "The change has taken place over the past 10 to 15 years because it was widely felt that mixing caused trouble and the two peoples needed to be separated if they were ever to live side-by-side."[4] This is in fact a rationalization for accepting P-B rather than P-A as the only worldview that is acceptable.

"When the Oslo peace process fell apart in 2000 and a Palestinian uprising erupted, the common wisdom that quickly developed was that the two nations needed not greater intimacy but complete separation. Israel built a barrier, barred most Palestinians from entering (replacing them with Asians on temporary visas) and made it illegal for Israeli citizens to enter Palestinian cities."[5] True wisdom would call for just the opposite behavior.

One strategy being used to promote peace which acknowledges the need for both compassion and Oneness is called Interpersonal Contact Theory. It is based on the principle that all human beings are fundamentally alike regardless of superficial differences (illusions of an *other*) such as skin color, religion, ethnicity, nationality, etc. This well-intentioned effort has faith in the natural compassion that is created when even just one person from each side of a conflict get to know one another.

The Seeds of Peace program brings together several hundred teenagers from conflict regions such as Israel and the Palestinian territories for a three-week summer camp in Maine. "The teenagers sleep, eat and play games together, and engage in daily sessions to talk about the conflict between their groups and their own experiences with it."[6] Unfortunately, this brief break from the poisonous context of their conflict-torn farms or villages is not enough to prevent a regression to the old worldview upon return home.

The vision that should guide all of us is that if we would allow ourselves to get to know each other we would find reasons for serious conflicts irrational. We are all neighbors after all living in a global village that would feel like paradise if we would only choose that belief rather than the fear-driven, Darwinian belief in the survival of the fittest.

Analysis of the Problems of War

Let's endeavor to understand that old poisonous context now and maybe we will be motivated to choose differently the next time we feel threatened by the non-existent *other*.

We shift our focus primarily to Americans who seem to be particularly fond of war although they would, of course, deny that. Skip this essay if you take umbrage at being labeled among the bellicose American homo saps. Those of us that value the truth will push on without you even though we may find the facts painful as we encounter them; not, however, as painful as the endless wars we are currently experiencing in the global village.

What's the evidence for what to some of you may seem to be tenuous claims regarding war and the U.S.? First, we are fond of war, at least many American males are. Secondly, our wars have become serial wars that, in modern times at least, never end; only a pause is necessary before we rationalize starting the next one. And finally, for a nation enamored of war, we are not very good at fighting them. The military-industrial complex, especially in Russia and the U.S. is, however, very good at manufacturing and marketing the weapons necessary to keep up the momentum of war, war, endless war.

General Incompetence

Let's take the last point in the previous paragraph first, i.e., that the U.S. is not very good at fighting wars, especially in the last 50 or 60 years. Dexter Filkins in a review of John Nagles *Knife Fights: A Memoir of Modern War in Theory and Practice* ends his essay with this assessment: "No matter how much time and effort and blood the United States expends, it has proved itself to be not very good at fighting guerilllas in faraway countries, and in setting up governments that endure. Counter-insurgency is an interesting theory, but the practice of it—at least the American practice of it—has been mostly a failure."[7]

What the U.S. is good at, albeit unconsciously, is creating terrorists. Recent American foreign policy and strategies of the Department of Defense in seeking to protect Americans from foreign and domestic terrorists have ended up aiding and abetting those we have targeted. In fact our erstwhile enemies characterize the *U.S.* as the terrorists; terrorists with lots of weapons and money. How do American policies create terrorists and insurgencies? Sarah Chayes in her insightful book *Thieves of State: Why Corruption Threatens Global Security* confirms what many of us have also observed. "Development resources passed through a corrupt system [in Afghanistan] not only reinforced that system by helping to fund it but also inflamed the feelings of injustice that were driving people toward the insurgency."[8]

The U.S. government and its people were playing patsy to criminals posing as legitimate public servants. The U.S. is good at this; we have had lots of practice. What we are not good at is sensing the long-term consequences of poorly thought-out survival strategies. "One key reason the United States and its allies have struggled to establish sustainable democracies in Afghanistan and Iraq is that the governments of those countries are mired in graft, caught in a mafia-like system in which money flows upward. The same goes for parts of Africa and Asia and most of the former Soviet Union."[9]

Now let's make the connection between the *naïve* U.S. foreign policy, corrupt foreign government officials, and the creation of terrorists and insurgencies. What Chayes calls a "basic fact" is one that we all need to become mindful of. With Chayes's extensive background as a journalist writing about U.S. foreign policy and its consequences, we need to heed her conclusion that "where there is poor governance—specifically, no appeal to the rule of law and no protected right of property—people begin a search for spiritual purity that puts them on a path to radicalization."[10] A suicide bomber is certainly a "radicalized" Islamist.

Macho Warriors

For many American males (and probably some females) their identity is confused with delusional images of achieving self-worth through acts of violence. "One could argue that wars are largely fueled by misshapen notions of honor and manhood."[11] Only recently have we begun to understand that war and human beings are absolutely incompatible and that courage and machismo are part of the illusion of the false self. "During World War I, traumatized soldiers were viewed as cowards, and 306 hysterical soldiers were shot; hundreds more were subjected to electric treatment. During the Vietnam War, such individuals were considered schizophrenics. In the 1970's one V.A. psychiatrist called the idea of PTSD an 'insult to brave men.'"[12]

War, War Forever More

One reason we accept the violence of war going back to the horrors faced by Homer's Achilles over 4,000 years ago is that we cope with war the same way we handle all our suffering, we engage in denial and distractions. We keep ourselves busy choosing the activities associated with the pursuit of plenty, pleasure and power. "No other people are as disconnected from the brutality of war as the United States is today."[13]

David Morris, a journalist and former Marine infantry officer writes in his book about Post-Traumatic Stress Disorder, about his frustration in getting Americans to acknowledge what his experience of war had been. "'The War had hurt me,' he writes, 'I wanted the country to feel some of that hurt.' Yet at home, he could barely begin to describe what he had seen because no one in America was listening. 'I realized that the problem wasn't just that they didn't want to understand it. What I had to say was not only inconvenient to their peace of mind but a tangible threat to it.'"[14]

The "good" thing about war is that it is the gift that keeps on giving; giving, that is, if the creation of suffering is the goal. The trauma suffered by the soldiers continues as many return to civilian life and begin to project their suffering on their families and communities. The damage of this trauma can be passed on for generations, raging through the lives of thousands in the community like a slow-motion tsunami sucking thousands out into the sea of despair, as they flail about confused and powerless. Such are the wages of war.

Let's not forget suicide. "By 2012, more American soldiers were killing themselves than were dying in combat. But the problem goes deeper beyond those in uniform. Suicide rates among American adults between 35 and 64 are at record rates as well, notes Dreazen [author of *The Invisible Front: Love and Loss in an Era of Endless War*], the managing editor of Foreign Policy and a former military affairs writer for The Wall Street Journal. He offers a sophisticated examination of an act of ultimate despair that irreversibly wounds the living and remains hidden, stigmatized and largely misunderstood."[15] Our inability to understand war and its consequences betrays a deeper dilemma; the inability to distinguish between illusion and reality.

The dilemma faced by Morris in the U.S. as he described it above parallels a much deeper challenge in the human community as a whole. The book you are reading is the fifth book in the Simple Reality Project, itself a lamentation on the reluctance of the average person to acknowledge what is *really* happening as opposed to what they *wished* were happening. The failure of the Simple Reality blog and books to connect with many people so far may indicate that the content is "inconvenient to their peace of mind" or "a tangible threat to it." We may continue to engage in denial and distraction, tell ourselves and others lies and pretend that we are keeping secret the quiet whispers of our True self, but we know better. Don't we! Yes, we do.

Just as humanity is avoiding the truth about war we are choosing, to our detriment, to deny the truth about reality itself. We are choosing instead the illusion of P-B and that is proving to be a fatal choice for the inhabitants of the communities of the global village.[1]

---

[1] More on the topic of War can be found in the *Simple Reality* published books and on the blog http://mysimplereality.com

We Can Do This

I am not writing for the applause of the moment, but for all time.
        Thucydides

The great chronicler of the Peloponnesian War between Athens and Sparta (431-404 B.C.E.) was committed to objectivity. However, objectivity is not possible in a world based on illusion. His so-called objective truth was simply not as Thucydides perceived it any more than the shimmering mirage of water exists on the hot highway in August.

In our own time the authors mentioned in this essay, sociologists rather than historians, were nevertheless committed to describing what they perceived and believed was happening in the American community. As we shall see, they did not have any more objectivity than did Thucydides. Something was indeed going on in Ancient Greece, but the unconscious human false self, assiduously committed or not, was not capable of knowing what that was. Nothing has changed in the interim. Something is happening in 21st century America, but we would be hard pressed to find many who know what that is.

During the 1950's several observers of American culture had insights into what they thought explained American behavior. "In *The Lonely Crowd*, published in 1950, David Riesman saw the emergence of "other-directed" patterns of social behavior, as different from the "inner-directed" patterns of earlier years."[1] Whatever patterns Riesman saw or imagined, he did not see anything remotely resembling authentic "inner-directed" behavior in an unconscious America. We are still searching for a connection to our inner wisdom found in the present moment. What Riesman would have had no trouble finding would have been delusional behavior patterns labeled the "Protestant work ethic," "rugged individualism," and "American exceptionalism."

William H. Whyte Jr. continued the examination of American manners and morals and unwittingly offered descriptions of how the bewildered and lost false self was behaving. What he was describing was how the collective unconscious in the U.S. determined the identity and behavior of Americans. In his book *The Organization Man,* he concluded "that representative Americans ... were becoming mass-organized conformists whose standards were not fixed or fundamental, but were shaped by shifting circumstances to those of their neighbors and business associates."[2] What Whyte's myopia and lack of awareness blocked him from seeing was that mass conformity had always been the basis for human behavior in human communities since those communities were first formed.

It is a natural (but unhealthy) reaction even for sociologists to project blame on the *other* for what they see to be self-destructive behavior. Just as political parties scapegoat "big government" today, "big business" provided a popular target for human suffering sixty years ago. Sloan Wilson's *The Man in the Gray Flannel Suit* (1955) spread anxiety about loss of autonomy in the workplace. "American men eager for success, for instance, wore gray flannel suits (or uniforms) ... and complied with regulations, prescribed by the large, paternalistic business corporations that controlled their futures."[3]

Sociologists as analysts seeking the truth of human behavior are as prone to projection as are the rest of us. They imagine causes or project their anxieties and prejudices onto the rest of us and those *seem* to explain behavioral trends in American society. For example, Logan Pearsall Smith defining "culture" missed a "defining" characteristic of reality itself although he unwittingly named it. "The indefatigable pursuit of an unattainable Perfection, even though it consist in nothing more than in the pounding of an old piano, is what alone gives meaning to our life on this unavailing star."[4] As long as we believe "perfection" to be unattainable it will be. Fish swimming in the ocean are unaware of and unappreciative of the perfect environment that nature has given them.

Those of us examining our community from the perspective of P-A see a much more hopeful future for America than the "chicken little" alarmists who fear the chaos of a collapsing global community. That hopeful future is possible only if we as a community decide to choose the True-self as our identity rather than the false self that academics, philosophers and some religious leaders are partial to. Optimism itself is also a choice as many of our insightful sages, who provided the content in the Simple Reality Project, have clearly indicated. The evidence for perfection is all around us, we are swimming in it.[m]

Many if not most intelligent and educated Americans are unable to distinguish illusion from reality. And yet we have reason for optimism regarding the creation of a sustainable community. The shattered paradigm that makes up the worldview of most Americans and our false-self identities derived from that delusional paradigm would seem to indicate that self-destructive behaviors will continue into the foreseeable future. True enough, however, just the existence of the choice available to all of us holds out the possibility of a change in direction. That choice is always being made by those more enlightened and insightful fish swimming right next to us, we simply are too lacking in awareness to see it. The life-enhancing principles of Simple Reality are nurturing people everywhere in the global village every moment of everyday.

Why can we do this, this in-our-face challenge of waking up? For two reasons. First, because we have the innate ability, the inner wisdom to guide us; and secondly, because it is not difficult. Waking up is not so much about doing as *not* doing; it is about choosing *not* to do a self-destructive thing and letting the healthy behavior naturally happen. True, we must learn discipline and self-restraint but we can all support each other in that respect. In fact many of us are already consciously expressing an alternative future for all of humanity.

---

[m] Refer to these essays and articles, among others, in the *Simple Reality* published books and on the blog http://mysimplereality.com.   • "The Collective Unconscious" • "Response and Reaction" • "Peak Experience" • "Compassion" • "The *Other*" • "Projection" • "Conditioning and Behavior Modification"

Response or Reaction:
Marshmallows, One or Two

In the 1960s and 1970s Stanford psychologist Walter Mischel conducted an experiment that captured the imagination of those searching for ways to empower children against the temptations of the false self, against the dead-end pursuit of plenty, pleasure and power. However, Mischel or anyone else would not have expressed this as the goal of his study of human behavior.

The results of Mischel's captivating experiment entitled "The Marshmallow Test" were revisited by the media in January 2014. What are the pundits excited about—what is The Marshmallow Test?[n]

Mischel's "test subjects" were 635 4-year-old preschool students at the Bing Nursery School on the Stanford campus. For follow-up studies in the 1980s Mischel and his colleagues were able to track down 185 of the original children. Today Mischel, now a professor at Columbia, has studied the brain activity of a small number of the original test subjects (now in their 40s) which show differing brain activity in those who were able to delay gratification and those who weren't. What do phrases like "delay gratification" mean? Good question.

Did we overstate in the previous essay the importance of discipline and self-restraint in creating a sustainable global village, or in the process of transformation, or in transcending pain and suffering? You be the judge because it is your life's experience that you are choosing each and every day.

---

[n] For more detail, refer to these articles: • "Marshmallows and Public Policy" by David Brooks, *The New York Times* • "Don't! The Secret of Self Control" by Jonah Lerner, *The New Yorker* • *"Just Let Them Eat the Marshmallow"* by Po Bronson, *The Daily Beast* • "Marshmallow Test—How Resisting a Sweet Can Lead to a Better Life" by Rebecca Camber, *The Daily Mail* • and many others

To create the context, let's go back to the original experiment. In Mischel's original study a researcher placed two marshmallows on the desk of each preschooler. They were told by the researcher that she had to leave the room for 15 or 20 minutes. They were also told that they could eat one marshmallow before she returned (but only one) or they could wait (exercising self-control) and eat both if they waited until she returned.[1]

Students of Simple Reality will recognize the appearance of the temptation to "react" or, resisting a conditioned trigger of the false-self sensation energy center and with a higher goal in mind, retain control of their emotions and "respond." Mischel nor his colleagues (either then or today) probably don't understand how profound the implications of the results are in what turned out to be a long-term study—originally not intended as such.

Daniel Goleman will help deepen our understanding of the significance of the behavior of the subjects in the experiment which he described in his book *Emotional Intelligence*. "There is perhaps no psychological skill more fundamental than resisting impulse. It is the root of all emotional self-control [and by extension, self-reliance], since all emotions, by their very nature, lead to one or another impulse to act [a reaction]. The root meaning of the word *emotion,* remember, is 'to move' … The marshmallow challenge … shows how fundamental is the ability to restrain the emotions [to respond or do nothing] and so delay impulse."[2]

What does this simple experiment involving marshmallows have to with building a healthier community over time? The worldview of the two groups of students was not the same nor was their identity. When they were revisited as adolescents the differences between the two groups had dramatic consequences. "Those who had resisted temptation at four were now, as adolescents, more socially competent: personally effective, self-assertive, and better able to cope with the frustrations of life. They were less likely to go to pieces, freeze, or regress under stress, or become rattled and disorganized when pressured; and they embraced challenges and pursued them instead of giving up even in the face of difficulties; they were self-reliant [Emerson would be pleased to hear this] and confident, trustworthy and dependable; and they took initiative and plunged into projects. And, more than a decade later, they were still able to delay gratification in pursuit of their goals."[3]

Those who had not waited and settled for one marshmallow had markedly different behavior than their more disciplined classmates as adolescents. "In adolescence they were more likely to be seen as shying away from social contacts; to be stubborn and indecisive; to be easily upset by frustrations; to think of themselves as 'bad' or unworthy; to regress or become immobilized by stress; to be mistrustful and resentful about not 'getting enough;' to be prone to jealousy and envy; to overreact to irritations with a sharp temper, so provoking arguments and fights. And, after all those years, they were still unable to put off gratification."[4]

I know, I know this all sound too good to be true. Surely we cannot train our children to have healthier behavior by simply teaching them about discipline and delayed gratification. But what makes a thing *true* in a given story or society? The *truth* is what we believe to be true and our belief in it gives it value and power to shape human behavior. We choose the components of our paradigm, our narrative; we decide what our beliefs, attitudes and values are going to be and weave them into a story about our community.

Could we teach our children the beliefs, attitudes and values that would empower them to consciously choose a response over a reaction and the specific skills and benefits related to delayed gratification? Of course we could. We could introduce them to The Point of Power Practice and the Simple Reality material.[o]

---

[o] More about the Point of Power Practice can be found in the Appendix of this book and in other *Simple Reality* published books, as well as on the blog http://mysimplereality.com

Choosing Compassion

Our sense of community in the U.S. is being lost and this is most obvious when we look at what other advanced democracies have achieved. In nations where public funds are used to pay for elections instead of private donors and PACs, lawmakers are free to respond to the needs of all voters from all economic classes not just the oligarchs.

"Strict gun safety laws, not dictated by gun maker lobbyists, increase kids' chances of living out their life spans. Child care benefits enable both moms and dads to work and raise stable families. Health care is guaranteed for all, without excessive profits to insurance and medical businesses. Higher education is subsidized, so graduates are free from huge college debt. Youths can get job apprenticeships in high schools, gaining skills to earn a living. Unions are accepted."[1] We have just read a description of communities where compassion is more in evidence than it is in the U.S.

Because of our immersion in P-B and the apparent reality of the world of form, including our own bodies, as the ultimate expression of our identity, the experience of our world seems anything but perfect. Probably few of us will be able to transcend this delusion but for those who can "feel" P-A when entering the ineffable present moment, we will not doubt our experience and we will have the insights to banish any doubt. One of the principles undergirding P-A is that of compassion, that is to say, serving and caring for others (including the *other*). In our community today, if we are alert, we can see the evidence of our neighbors' compassion being made manifest.

Compassion, one of the inherent aspects of the inner wisdom possessed by every human being, often lies dormant because the American narrative is more supportive of the behaviors surrounding the pursuit of plenty, pleasure and power, and competition over cooperation. But any of us can experience the insights of an awakening True self and change from reactive to responsive behaviors. For example, Barbara Bush, the daughter of President George W. Bush, was arrested for underage drinking in 2001. (Her father had surrendered to the same temptation during his "formative" years.)

We all come to many crossroads during our lifetimes and these are opportunities for a change in direction if not a shift in paradigm. Enough of these conscious choices, electing a response instead of a reaction, can add up to an awakening, a profound transformation in both our story and our identity.

In 2003, Barbara Bush accompanied her father on a trip to Africa. She was shocked by the human toll of AIDS in Uganda. This was her crossroads opportunity. She could have continued her narrative of self-medication expressing the sensation energy center of her false self. Instead of staying focused on her personal pain and suffering she "felt" the possibility of the genuine satisfaction in helping others.

"So she returned to Yale and took health classes, and then quietly took a job (while her father was still in the White House) in a South African hospital, often working with children with AIDS."[2] With five friends, she started Global Health Corps. She became chief executive at age 26. Today (2015) Global Health Corps receives 6,000 applications for less than 150 positions.

"'I'm a big fan of the Global Health Corps,' said Dr. Peter Piot, who helped discover Ebola and later ran the United Nations program on AIDS. 'They engage nonmedical people in global health'—and that, he said, is a central challenge of health care worldwide."[3]

Whatever Americans think of the controversial presidency of "W," his best legacy may be the example he set for his daughter in expressing his own True self. He responded to the AIDS crisis with his program called Pepfar which has saved millions of lives. Why are acts of compassion and programs like those started by Barbara Bush and her father not more common in the American community?

For Love or Money

What if a drug was discovered that was effective in the treatment of anxiety (including the fear experienced by terminally ill cancer patients facing death), alcohol and tobacco addiction, and depression—one that Thomas R. Insel, the director of the National Institute of Mental Health and a neuroscientist, thinks should be studied? But what if, despite its promise, it isn't being produced or marketed by Big Pharma. Don't we as a community have compassion for all those who suffer and could be helped? Insel has the answer when he reminds us that "it would be very difficult to get a pharmaceutical company interested in developing this drug, since it cannot be patented."[1] Or in the language of economists, it can't be "monetized;" profit first, empathy second.

Another problem with the drug is that it is too effective. Anthony Bossis, a psychologist at N.Y.U., pointed out that "there's not a lot of money here when you can be cured with one session."[2] One would think this drug is new and needs more study but that is not the case. Stanislov Groff, a former professor at Johns Hopkins University School of Medicine, has been studying this drug since the 1960s. He has written many books extolling the potential benefits of LSD. Yes, LSD. Surprised?

It would seem that in America where Big Pharma is concerned and compassion is in short supply, when the choice is love or money, if you're suffering, you're out of luck. Oh! You want to know what these hallucinogens and/or drugs in general have to do with Simple Reality? O.K. that is a reasonable request.

In 1953 Humphrey Osmond, an English psychiatrist, introduced Aldous Huxley to mescaline and it was Huxley who conceived of giving the drug to people who were dying. Osmond coined the term "psychedelic" which means "mind manifesting." In 1963 Huxley, dying of laryngeal cancer, had his wife inject him with the drug when he was on his deathbed. The author of *Brave New World* experienced and learned something we would do well to revisit today.

LSD was discovered by accident by Dr. Albert Hoffman in Switzerland and was recognized as the most potent of the consciousness-changing drugs. "Not an opiate or a narcotic, LSD is a chemical able to produce profound changes of consciousness which, in healthily constituted persons, seem to leave no untoward after effects. And while it can give an ecstatic experience, at the same time it lends an extraordinary intensity of attention."[3] Did the mystic Gerald Heard mean in that last sentence that LSD could heighten present moment awareness?

As Heard continues, notice how he seems to be describing Oneness, the present moment and the experience of the "observer" that many of us have in our meditations. "Time appears to have stopped, disappeared. What has now befallen the 'voyager' is not merely that he is on the high seas with his ship in a vast calm, but that the ship itself no longer seems distinct from the infinite ocean. He stands outside of and apart from his familiar ego [false-self], all its protective barriers [reactive survival strategy] having been shed; and this can lead in some to transcendence experience [awakening], while in others to a deep panic. To those for whom the ego is their only possible self, the only possible mode of consciousness, its disappearance is a kind of death."[4]

We should note that most of the experimenters cited in this essay are operating in the context of P-B with their false self evaluating the results. The conditions are such that an objective and profound understanding of the altered state of consciousness they achieved is unlikely. For a person already focusing on creating a new identity in a supportive context, the LSD experience can be much more positive. "It is true that mystics and saints have reported time and again, 'out-of-this-world,' indescribable experiences that did change their lives and bring a 'better order' in their living."[5] In other words their experiences were transformational in a positive way. How many of our heavily used drugs today offer such benefits?

Groff, a Czech-born psychiatrist, used LSD extensively in his practice in the 60s and 70s. Pioneers with open minds like Huxley and Groff had the courage to explore the unknown. Why don't we know more about their obviously promising discoveries?

Alas, in this country the Nixon administration shut down psychedelic research 40 years ago. Why?

The answer might be similar to why the content of Simple Reality is also not connecting with fear-driven Americans. Roland Griffiths, a psychopharmacologist at Johns Hopkins University School of Medicine explains why America's paternalistic leadership might not want psychedelics used as "medicine." "There is such a sense of authority that comes out of the primary mystical experience that it can be threatening to existing hierarchical structures. We ended up demonizing these compounds. Can you think of another area of science regarded as so dangerous and taboo that all research gets shut down for decades? It's unprecedented in modern science."[6]

It's not as if there are other conventional psychiatric drugs that are as effective in treating existential anxiety, not Prozac, not Xanax. Bossis said, "People don't realize how few tools we have in psychiatry to address existential distress ... So how can we not explore this, if it can recalibrate how we die?"[7] How indeed?

Not surprisingly, psychiatric drugs like Prozac affect the P-B "world of form" by altering long-term brain chemistry not by empowering the patient to undertake his own transformation.

The Pahnke-Richards Mystical Experience Questionnaire does evaluate the effect of psychedelics in a P-A context. "The questionnaire measures feelings of unity [Oneness], sacredness, ineffability, peace and joy, as well as the impression of having transcended space and time and the "noetic sense" that the experience is one that exhibits all six characteristics."[8]

We have to ask what percentage of those taking psychedelics have these experiences which were based in part on the descriptions in William James' *The Varieties of Religious Experience* written in 1902. In other words we Americans have had quite some time to investigate the possibility that we don't know everything about the power of transcendence, our ability to distinguish reality from illusion.

Griffiths also said, "I don't want to use the word 'mindblowing' ... but, as a scientific phenomenon, if you can create conditions in which seventy per cent of people will say they have had one of the five most meaningful experiences of their lives? To a scientist, that's just incredible."[9]

In April 2010 Patrick Mettes, a 54-year-old television news director, learned he had lung cancer (which ultimately caused his death). He saw a front-page article in the *Times* headlined HALLUCINOGENS HAVE DOCTORS TUNING IN AGAIN. Toward the end of his life, a few years later, he described his experience and was glad he consented to use those hallucinogens. "From here on, love was the only consideration. It was and is the only purpose. Love seemed to emanate from a single point of light ... no sensation, no image of beauty, nothing during my time on earth has felt as pure and joyful and glorious as the height of this journey."[10]

What about the more objective observations of others in the room with Mettes, Dr. Bossis, for example: "'You're in this room, but you're in the presence of something large,' he recalled, 'it's humbling to sit there. It's the most rewarding day of your career.'"[11] So perhaps when we learn to choose the identity that values love more than money, it will be much more than a rewarding day.

Religion or No Religion?
That Is the Question. Whether Tis Nobler ...
Blah, Blah Blah ...

If there is a worldview that appreciates the futility of using the intellect to answer profound questions, it is Zen. "Zen masters sternly reject all the speculation, ratiocination, and verbalism so dear to the intellectual Westerner."[1] A 1959 article "The Square Roots of Zen" in *Horizon* magazine reveals how recently Americans were introduced to this exotic arrival from Japan. "During the last few years in America a small Japanese word, with a not inappropriate buzzing and stinging sound, has begun to be heard in casual or earnest reference in very unlikely places: at ladies' luncheons, on serious academic platforms, at cocktail parties, and in campus hangouts."[2]

What was Zen understood to be over 50 years ago other than "exotic." "Sometimes called a religion, sometimes referred to as 'the religion of no-religion,' sometimes identified simply as a 'way of life,' Zen's origins are extremely ancient and its modern Western blooming as a phenomenon with both positive and negative sides."[3] We will find that Zen is nothing more than Simple Reality wearing a monk's robe and having a good time celebrating the joy of life. For Westerners this is all more than a little confusing. We can straighten it out because after all, it's really very simple.

Daisetz Teitara Suzuki first came to the U.S. in 1897, has taught at many universities here and authored more than a score of books about Zen. The name Daisetz, given to him by a Zen master—means "great stupidity,"—but the true meaning is "great simplicity." Here is our first Simple Reality principle, along with the rest of the formula, which when translated into Algebra reads:

S + S + S = S
Simplicity + Solitude + Silence = Serenity

This foundation is one that we will all want to put into place before we begin our process of self-transformation.

We said that Zen and Simple Reality are simple, but we didn't say they are easy. The reason that both the practice of Zen and The Point of Power Practice attract so few adherents is that the barriers created during our years of behavioral conditioning are formidable. The narrative in which we are contained and our resulting identity, our beliefs, attitudes and values are like a vast landscape of stubborn and burgeoning weeds with deep roots in the subterranean subconscious.

Don't lose heart, we can do this. More Simple Reality principles found in Zen teachings: "By definite methods of instruction Zen strives to bring about *direct intuitive perception* [by-passing the intellect] on the part of each individual seeker."[4] Self–transformation is accomplished by insights with Oneness being the prerequisite realization. "There is now deeply sensed that secret 'rhythm of life' flowing eternally through all things and creatures, that immanent spirit or essence."[5]

Meditation plays a central role in the practice of Zen and as we say in Simple Reality "our life *becomes* a meditation." "The duties and enjoyments of ordinary human existence are carried on quite as usual, only now there is evident a new serenity and balance, more simplicity about one's mode of living, and above all, more 'detachment' from the strains, annoyances, and anxieties of everyday affairs."[6]

We should not be surprised to see that the word "experience" looms large in the tenets of Zen. After all it was Buddha who said that the purpose of meditation was to experience reality as it *really* is. "The key to realization lies in the words 'direct immediate experience,' or 'direct seeing into reality [insight].' The condition of enlightenment [waking up] itself and not words about that condition are what truly matter in Zen."[7] How do we do that?

- First of all, we must re-direct our energy and that is done by making different choices.
- Secondly, we must commit whatever energy is necessary to overcome the inertia of our reactive false self. One must work out one's own salvation "with diligence," as Buddha said.

- And finally, one must attain *satori*, the present moment, by choosing not to react all day long, day in and day out. "The truth should be understood through sudden enlightenment but the fact is that the complete realization must be cultivated step by step."[8]

If we continue to choose money (a reaction) instead of compassion (a response), fear instead of joy, then we will continue to move in the direction of doom, engaging in diversion, denial, and distraction, resulting in despair. The continuum of human behavior is Utopia to Dystopia. In which direction are you headed?

CHAPTER 3
THE FUTURE OF THE HUMAN COMMUNITY

The Robotic False Self

In the context of Simple Reality we have used robots as metaphors for the false self. Now it seems the two are beginning to meld into one another. Could it be true that in the future we may not be able to tell "Hal" from Harold, "Her" from Harriet?

A psychopathological robot like Hal made for good entertainment in a Hollywood sci-fi film, but surely robots are no threat to us because we make them, we program them—right? What a relief! We can all relax. But wait! Who is the "we" that programs them? Oh Oh! It is the false self. Hello Houston—we have a problem.

Nicholas Carr, former executive editor of the *Harvard Business Review* and author of several books on technology, in his book *The Shallows,* pointed out that the Web has had a detrimental effect on our ability to read, think and reflect. In his new book *The Glass Cage: Automation and Us,* Carr explains "how certain aspects of automotive technology can separate us from, well, Reality."[1] Here is our first clue of how robots and the false self are becoming indistinguishable. The false self's survival strategy behaviors are precisely what prevents us from experiencing Simple Reality. We created the false self expressly to distract us from living in the present moment. Let's continue this fascinating analysis.

What we know about most of us is that we seek activities that will distract us from our pain and suffering and conversely avoid behavior that allows us to be aware of what's really happening in our lives—especially activities associated with simplicity, solitude and silence—we will avoid introspection at all costs. "In 11 experiments involving more than 700 people, the majority of participants reported that they found it unpleasant to be alone in a room with their thoughts for just 6 to 15 minutes."[2]

> *All humanity's problems can be traced to our inability to sit alone in a room for 15 minutes.*
> Pascal

There is nothing funny about our inability to begin the process of waking up but comedian Louis C. K. has managed to create a riff watched more than eight million times on YouTube that zeroes in on what it feels like to not be comfortable in our own skin—our false-self skin, that is. "'Sometimes when things clear away and you're not watching anything and you're in your car and you start going, oh no, here it comes, that I'm alone, and it starts to visit on you, just this sadness,' he said. 'And that's why we text and drive. People are willing to risk taking a life and ruining their own because they don't want to be alone for a second because it's so hard."[3]

Psychologist Stephanie Brown, author of *Speed: Facing Our Addiction to Fast* and *Faster and Overcoming Our Fear of Slowing Down,* says "There's this widespread belief that thinking and feeling will only slow you down and get in your way, but it's the opposite."[4] Actually, as we have learned from our sages, it *is* thinking and feeling (as in emotions) that block our entering the present moment where we could actually put our mind at rest. How ironic!

Aided and abetted by our devices we seem to have stepped onto a treadmill that continually accelerates, or as some would say we have "stepped onto a slippery slope." Working to quiet our "mind chatter," to medicate the symptoms showing up in our bodies and to distract ourselves from our afflictive emotions only serves to push us to continually work harder to suppress those reactions and give them more power over our behavior.

Even former technology enthusiasts like Sherry Turkle are forced to acknowledge the evidence that continues to pile up that makes us ask the question, who is really in control of human behavior? "She holds an endowed chair at M.I.T. and is on close collegial terms with the roboticists and affective-computing engineers who work there."[5]

In her latest book, *Reclaiming Conversation: The Power of Talk in a Digital Age,* she gains insights through interviews on how social media are affecting the beliefs, attitudes and values of Americans enamored of their devices. Reviewing her book, Jonathan Franzen reveals one of her conclusions. "Our rapturous submission to digital technology has led to an atrophying of human capacities like empathy and self-reflection ... The people she interviews have adopted new technologies in pursuit of greater control, only to feel controlled by them."[6]

Again we have to remind our readers that it is not our beloved and much coveted devices which give us the illusion of control that is problematic, but the false-self *need* to be in control of that which cannot be controlled (and doesn't need to be controlled) that is the source of our shrinking ability to access our compassion for one another. "A recent study shows a steep decline in empathy, as measured by standard psychological tests, among college students of the smartphone generation."[7]

What are we beginning to realize about our much vaunted intellect and its ability to mesmerize us with its marvelous technology? "How, for all its miraculous-seeming benefits, automation also can and often does impair our mental and physical skills, cause dreadful mistakes and accidents, particularly in medicine and aviation, and threaten to turn the algorithms we create as servants into our mindless masters—what sci-fi movies have been warning us about for at least two or three decades now. (As Carr puts it near the end of *The Glass Cage,* when we become dependent on our technological slaves ... we turn into slaves ourselves.)"[8]

How does technology adversely affect our physical health? In 2005, the RAND Corporation predicted that electronic medical records could save more than $81 billion annually but it turns out that the computer screen interposes itself between the patient and the doctor with a detrimental effect. "Studies have proved that checking records, possible diagnoses and drug interactions on a computer during a medical examination can interfere with what should be not only a fact-based investigation but a deeply human, partly intuitive and empathetic process."[9] When our technology begins to reduce the ability of our doctors to respond to their patients in the present moment with compassion—that should cause us to pause—are we headed in the right direction?

Now to the implications for aviation. Pilots are becoming increasingly dependent on automated flying. "A heavy reliance on computer automation can erode a pilot's expertise ... leading to what Jan Noyes, a human-factors expert at Britain's University of Bristol, calls 'a deskilling of the crew.'"[10] When a key principle involved in human awakening is self-reliance, then dependence on robots is clearly self-limiting and ultimately self-destructive.

Are we being too pessimistic or even paranoid about Artificial Intelligence? Tesla's chief executive Elon Musk suggests proceeding carefully with the development of A.I. "just to make sure that we don't do something very foolish."[11]

Bill Gates said he didn't "understand why some people are not concerned [about] super intelligence."[12] Stephen Hawking sounds the most piercing alarm by scientists who are concerned about the possibility of a dark side to developing human-like robots. He warned that "the development of full artificial intelligence could spell the end of the human race."[13] Is Stephen Hawking overreacting? Probably not, as we shall see.

John Markoff, author of *Machines of Loving Grace: The Quest for Common Ground Between Humans and Robots,* seems to share Hawking's concern. "The same technologies that extend the intellectual power of humans can displace them as well."[14]

Even something so apparently harmless as a child's doll can morph into a threatening A.I. toy in the hands of a false self intent on making a profit. The doll officially named Barbara Millicent Roberts or "Barbie" made her appearance at the New York Toy Fair in 1959. With over a billion dollars in sales and a "fandom" of millions of little girls, what could be the problem? Well, for starters: "Protestors at the 1972 Toy Fair complained that Barbie and other dolls encouraged girls 'to see themselves solely as mannequins, sex objects or housekeepers,' according to an account in *The New York Times.*"[15]

"A 2006 study in the journal Developmental Psychology bluntly concluded that 'girls exposed to Barbie reported lower body esteem and greater desire for a thinner body shape."[16] If that's not enough cause for alarm wait until we see what Mattel is up to now. What if the toymaker could create the illusion that Barbie was a sentient being? Introducing "Hello Barbie" in her latest new and improved incarnation. But first a little background story on the interface between toys, dolls and A.I.

"In the 1960s, a computer scientist, Joseph Weizenbaum, created a computer program called Eliza, which could pretend to be a psychotherapist via a simple text interface. As Weizenbaum later wrote, 'I was startled to see how quickly and how very deeply people ... became emotionally involved with the computer and how unequivocally they anthropomorphized it."[17] We have just introduced the problem facing all of humanity in our attempts to create a sustainable human community, namely, what's real and what isn't or in this example, what's human and what isn't?

M.I.T. roboticists Cynthia Breazeal and Brian Scassellati along with psychologist Sherry Turkle introduced children to the robots Cog and Kismet in 2001. The robots, unlike Hello Barbie, couldn't speak but engaged the children through eye contact, gestures and facial expressions. The researchers pulled aside the curtain to reveal that it was "The Wizard of Oz" operating the deceptively real robots by showing the children how the robots worked and letting them control the robots. Nevertheless "most children said they believed that Kismet and Cog could listen, feel, care about them and make friends."[18]

Imagine how lifelike Hello Barbie will seem to a 3 to 8-year-old with her 8,000 lines of realistically responsive dialogue. In the late 1990s, Noel Sharkey, a professor at the University of Sheffield in England was studying the interface of robotics and ethics. His daughter ended up being strongly attached to her robot Tamagotchi. "We had to break it away from my daughter in the end, because she was obsessed with it. It was like, 'Oh, my God, my Tamagotchi is going to die."[19]

Mattel will not be trying to cause our children psychological problems with Hello Barbie but in the understandable need to make a profit, the toy manufacturer may be fostering unintended consequences. To sell more dolls we can trust that Mattel will use A.I. technologies to make the doll more likeable. "The first thing you're going to do is to try and create stronger and stronger emotional bonds." The danger is that a synthetic friendship may take the place of the real kind. Sharkey continues,

"If you've got someone who you can talk to all the time, why bother making friends."[20]

University of Washington professor of psychology, Peter Kahn, studies human-robot interaction and defines the "domination model" relationship in which the child makes all the demands and receives all the rewards but feels no responsibility to the robot. In other words, the robot becomes a kind of A.I. *other*. "This, he says, is unhealthy for moral and emotional development. At worst, the human can begin to abuse his power. In a study conducted at a Japanese shopping mall a couple of years ago, for instance, researchers videotaped numerous children who kicked and punched a humanoid robot when it got in their way."[21]

How do we teach children to distinguish between illusion and reality when we adults have yet to grasp the difference? Remember that a person's identity is determined by their worldview and that our worldview is composed of our BELIEFS, attitudes and values. Psychologist Sherry Turkle completes our circle. "It's not that we have really invented machines that love us or care about us in any way, shape or form, but that we are ready to BELIEVE [emphasis added] that they do. We are ready to play their game."[22]

Speaking of games, IBM's A.I. system called "Watson" defeated human champions in the quiz show game "Jeopardy" in 2011. Like Mattel, IBM wants to find ways to commercialize this A.I. technology. "On Thursday [September 24, 2015], IBM announced new capabilities in Watson services like speech [Hello Watson?], language understanding, image recognition and sentiment analysis. These humanlike abilities such as seeing, listening and reasoning are those associated with artificial intelligence in computing. IBM calls its approach to A.I. 'cognitive computing.'"[23]

It is obviously easier to program a computer to emulate the human intellect (cognitive computing) than human affective behavior. We should all be concerned that we don't create a form of A.I. that lacks our best human qualities such as morality and compassion. Which begs the question, just how much morality and compassion is being expressed around the global village today? Not much, regrettably. Perhaps we could program a robot to better express our True self than we ourselves have been able to do so far in our history of human interaction. What would that entail?

"Computer scientists are teaming up with philosophers, psychologists, linguists, lawyers, theologians and human rights experts to identify the set of decision points that robots would need to work through in order to emulate our own thinking about right and wrong. Scheutz [Matthias Scheutz of the Human-Robot Interaction Laboratory at Tufts University] defines "morality" broadly, as a factor that can come into play when choosing between contradictory paths."[24]

Simple Reality empowers humans to choose between the contradictory "paths" of reaction and response in order to express morality and compassion, in order to create a sustainable community. Perhaps robots could be programmed to distinguish between self-destructive behavior and life-enhancing behavior. If so then A.I. may be able to support humanity in making the paradigm shift that seems to be our only hope for survival.

Just kidding! If you took that last sentence seriously you are not paying attention to the content found in the Simple Reality Project. You are grasping at straws. In P-B there are two so-called "paths," neither of which lead anywhere and the "leaders" beckoning us to follow them are in conventional religious terms Satan (Christianity) or Maya (Buddhism), or in technological terms Artificial Intelligence (A.I.). Neither religion nor the human intellect hold out any hope because they are both creations of our P-B identity.

Anthropomorphism is the great seducer in both cases described above. As robots become more human-like, as they obviously will, we will be tempted to surrender more of our agency to them and shrink from both our responsibility and our opportunity to become self-reliant and to engage in the process of authentic transformation, which is the only true power that we have and the only power that we need. If we listen to our false self, our robots will become more anthropomorphic as we become more like robots.

On the other hand, if we continue to listen to pseudo-religious leaders invoking the divine illusion of an anthropomorphic God, we will also continue to stagger forward, sleepwalking toward chaos and the collapse of civilization. Our false-self will continue to project our anxiety, guilt, shame and regret on the "Sky God" or the blameless *other* living next door.

The Implicate Order[p] (Creative Intelligence) can be trusted to guide us in expressing our True self if we reject reaction and embrace response. In doing so we embrace the perfection of Creation and we ourselves become creators of both Truth and Beauty.

---

[p] More about the Implicate Order can be found in *Simple Reality* published books and on the blog http://mysimplereality.com

What Future?

The musical "South Pacific," based on James Michener's book, has a song lyric about a "cockeyed optimist" who is "immature and incurably green." Or we might say "sentimental" or "nostalgic" when it comes to looking back at human history. What about looking *forward* into the future of the human community? Is there cause for optimism?

Angus Deaton in his book *The Great Escape: Health, Wealth, and the Origins of Inequality* seems to think that things are getting better and will continue to improve for the inhabitants of the Global Village. In fact, he thinks that things began to improve for humanity in the 18th century with the Enlightenment. This was when it could be said that humans began to think rationally and began to transcend dogma and superstition. Is he right? Are things looking up for humankind?

"Life expectancy has risen a stunning 50 percent since 1900 and is still rising. Despite the resulting population explosion, the average quality of life has surged. The share of people living on less than $1 a day (in inflation-adjusted terms) has dropped to 14 percent, from 42 percent as recently as 1981. Even as inequality has surged within many countries, global inequality has very likely fallen, thanks largely to the rise of Asia. 'Things are getting better,' he writes, 'and hugely so.'"[1] Things *seem* to be getting better for most of the people on earth who can look forward to a better quality of life. The operational word in that last sentence is *seems*.

In the global village where self-delusion is universal, it is not a good idea to make decisions or solve problems based on what *appears* to be happening rather than on what is *actually* happening. In his book, Deaton focused on long-term historical trends. If he is correct, then people in general would be expressing more satisfaction, happiness and peace of mind. Are they?

People in the U.S. should be enjoying the benefits of prosperity and technology. Right? "It has long held true that elderly people have higher suicide rates than the overall population. But numbers released in May [2013] by the Centers for Disease Control and Prevention show a dramatic spike in suicides among middle-aged people, with the highest increases among men in their 50s, whose rate went up by nearly 50 percent to 30 per 100,000; and women in their early 60s, whose rate rose by nearly 60 percent (although it is still relatively low compared with men, at 7 in 100,000)."[2] Of course, we must look more broadly at other behaviors before we can draw any general conclusions.

"Compared with their parents' generation, boomers have higher rates of obesity, prescription and illicit drug abuse, alcoholism, divorce, depression and mental disorders. As they age, many add to that list chronic illness, disabilities and the strains of caring for their parents and for adult children who still depend on them financially."[3] Our conclusion? The quality of life in America is getting worse not better and the rest of the world is the same differing only in the details. In other words, the future is bleak unless we begin to make some changes—profound shifts, not cosmetic changes.

Trust is an all-important component of our belief system that influences quality of life for those in a community; without trust, change is difficult. The more people we believe to be the *other*, or less human or less trustworthy than *we* are, the less compassion we feel for them and the more threatened we are by them. Acceptance and compassion must be growing in any community that expects to have a future worth living. One name that sociologists have for this quality in a community is "social trust."

In a healthy forward-looking community people are willing to work with and trust those who are different from them. Any community that is going to have a successful future must see all members of the community as essentially the same and all will work in harmony for the common good.

Unfortunately, in America, trust and harmony are decreasing. "For four decades, a gut-level ingredient of democracy—trust in the other fellow—has been quietly draining away. These days only one-third of Americans say most people can be trusted. Half felt that way in 1972, when the General Social Survey first asked the question."4

Central to understanding whether a given society is making progress is how people behave towards each other in general. We have learned that a key measure of human behavior is the ratio of responses to reactions. In a community that is making progress toward enhanced mental and physical health, community members will be more responsive or compassionate toward one another. April K. Clark, a Purdue University political scientist and public opinion researcher describes the role that trust has in a community. "'It's like the rules of the game,' Clark said. 'When trust is low, the way we react and behave with each other becomes less civil.'"5 Yes, civility in America is, unfortunately, on the wane.

There is cause for alarm in the U.S. as we make our descent toward chaos, but there are other societies farther down that slippery slope and they in a sense are giving us a preview of our own darker tomorrows. We want desperately to believe things can and are getting better within nations that seem to have made promising beginnings at solving long-standing problems. We will use India as an example of the wishful thinking that only prolongs our acceptance of the truth.

Those of us prone to grasp at straws to alleviate our anxiety are susceptible to delusion and denial. We are quick to look at the success of India's elite and project that upon the Indian society as a whole. They have their "gated communities" just as we in America do. These so-called green zones are where Indian professionals mimic a first-world economy behind walls and security checkpoints.

For example, the Hiranandani brothers who are billionaire real estate developers, are behind the Contractor project in Mumbai. It houses more than 15,000 people, offices for more than 150 companies and includes its own schools, hospital and recreational facilities. "At Hiranandani Gardens, you can almost forget you're in a nation where 300 million people lack electricity. You certainly don't have to worry about bathroom lines. Inside Hiranandani Gardens—taking a meeting at Colgate

Palmolive, including lunch at Pizza Hut—there is little, save the auto-rickshaws buzzing down Technology Street, to remind you that you're even in India. And that is precisely the point."[6] Hiranandani Gardens like many such projects around the world are merely houses of straw waiting to be blown away by the tornadic winds of reality.

Those winds of reality are driven by the human false self and its lust for plenty, pleasure and power. In Delhi beginning in 2000 the false-self survival strategy was much in evidence, corruption was rampant. "The land grabs and corruption-as-usual that became so blatant ... the extension of the power of elites at the cost of everyone else, the conversion of all that was slow, intimate and idiosyncratic into the fast, vast and generic—it made it difficult to dream of surprising futures any more ... even as people made more money, things made less sense."[7]

Even though the approaching "future" chaos may appear to be happening in different ways in different parts of the world it is all part of one systemic expression of unconsciousness. Both the slum dwellers and the elite are trapped in a narrative in which only the details of their suffering and self-destruction differ. Not only is progress of any kind on our planet an illusion, the very concept of any "future" is a gross self-deception. More on that in a moment.

Back to one last glimpse of Mumbai. Jean Dreze and Amartya Sen in their best seller *An Uncertain Glory: India and Its Contradictions,* reveal that it is not first-world capitalism that will save India from chaos. "'There is a real need for pragmatism here,' they write, 'and to avoid both the crushing inefficiency of market denial ... and the pathology of ideological marketization.'"[8]

Remember our operational word in our desperate search for a positive future—the good news is perhaps not what it *seems*—what we should be searching for is the truth. The elite appear to be doing well in Mumbai or in Delhi but they are inseparably connected to the rest of the people in India, their walls and malls notwithstanding. Dreze and Sen are the realists. "They show that, leaving aside per capita income, which has grown impressively, India is actually falling behind its neighbors in South Asia—never mind America, Europe and China—in every social indicator that matters, from literacy to child malnutrition to access to toilets. In fact, large numbers of Indian primary-school students are unable to write a simple sentence or do basic arithmetic."[9] Inescapable conclusion: Americans and Indians are in the same boat heading toward the Niagara Falls of our collective future.

But wait—in this essay we are saying that we have no future. What do we mean by that?

The examples of human behavior we have used are the universal expression of the pursuit of plenty, pleasure and power by individuals with their false-self identities. These behaviors are reactions to the shame, guilt and regret as they imagine themselves in the past, or reactions to an imagined future that is causing them anxiety. The problem with these very common reactions is that they are not occurring in the present moment which is the only time and place where our lives *can* happen.

There is no future for humanity because nothing happens in an imagined future, it only happens in the Now. We either learn to choose to stop resisting our life, our experience, by responding to what is happening or we can unconsciously choose to flee from what *seems* to be happening into a non-existent past or future and spend our lives asleep.

Ironically, the only future we have is the experience we choose to create in the present moment. The good news is that we don't have to wait for that future, we can create it *NOW*.

Cockeyed Optimist

from the musical South Pacific
By Rogers & Hammerstein

When the sky's a bright canary yellow
I forget every cloud I've ever seen,
So they call me a cockeyed optimist
Immature and incurably green.

I've heard people rant and rave and bellow
That we're done and we might as well be dead,
But I'm only a cockeyed optimist
And I can't get it into my head.

I hear the human race
Is falling on it's face
And hasn't very far to go,
But ev'ry whippoorwill
Is selling me a bill,
And telling me it just ain't so.

I could say life is just a bowl of Jello
And appear more intelligent and smart,
But I'm stuck like a dope
With a thing called hope,
And I can't get it out of my heart!
Not this heart

CHAPTER 4
INSIGHTS— COMMUNITY AND SIMPLE REALITY

Absurdity

We meet our destiny on the road we take to avoid it.
    C. G. Jung

In P-B most of us exist in a meaningless and irrational universe in which our life, if we have the courage to be honest, makes no sense and has no discernible purpose. We have become the dictionary definition of ridiculous, incongruous and unreasonable. And yet we persist. Why?

The truth is that we create our own reality and we can do so unconsciously or with an awareness of why we do what we do. Therefore, to continue to create an unsatisfactory experience and then go into afflictive reaction to that experience is an exercise in absurdity. We can learn to give a deep and resonant meaning to our lives or as Deepak Chopra put it: "Today I will accept people, situations, circumstances, and events as they occur. This means I will know that this moment is as it should be, because the whole universe is as it should be."[1]

An example of the how ridiculous false-self driven behavior can become is revealed in this anecdote about George Steinbrenner relating to the 1978 Yankees-Red Sox playoff game. Steinbrenner chewed out Al Rosen for losing the coin toss. How's that for being unclear about the nature of reality.[2]

As mystics (those who experience the present moment) we have the opportunity to become creative teachers by passing along and/or modeling the principles of Simple Reality. For example, as perfect individuals within a perfect creation, we surely regard the notion of sin as absurd. It is indeed nonsensical as is this easy-to-remember acronym suggests: SIN=Self-Imposed Nonsense.

After we have all had a good laugh observing our nonsensical, and at times comical behavior, we can begin the joy-filled process of learning to respond to the wonderful life we have been given with rational, compassionate and wholesome behaviors. Then the only absurdity about our behavior would be, why did we take so long to do this?

Cooperation and Competition

Overemphasis on the competitive system and premature specialization on the grounds of immediate usefulness kill the spirit on which all cultural life depends, specialized knowledge included.
    Albert Einstein

The values of P-B permeate the institutions that are themselves an expression of the collective worldview of a society. Competition is often an expression of fear in P-B and can have a toxic effect as Albert Einstein observed. Rick Fields agrees with Einstein: "Modern education is competitive, rationalistic and separative. It has trained the child to regard material values as of major importance, to believe that his nation is also of major importance and superior to other nations and peoples. The general level of world information is high but usually biased, influenced by national prejudices, serving to make us citizens of our nation but not of the world."[1]

Artificial fragmentation or "splits" of the unitary world of form, which are illusions within our mind, will lead to self-destructive behavior because they create and sustain fear. Our belief that we live in a story which demands that we commit much of our energy to competition also intensifies that energy we express as fear.

However, competition per se is not the problem but rather the influence of the P-B narrative that contains it. How are winning and losing experienced from a P-A perspective? Sakyong Mipham Rinpoche has some valuable insights. "When we compete, we are honing our skills of aggression. In abstaining from a competitive state of mind, we are taking confidence in our worthiness as a human being who can cultivate wisdom and compassion. We appreciate others. When they outperform us, we don't see it as belittlement, but as an opportunity to relax into the outrageous possibility of not being attached to gain and loss. Gain and loss are meaningless preoccupations that we use to foster the illusion of a permanent self."[2]

The American culture seems to have surrendered to the "survival of the fittest" belief system more than have of other nations in the West. "The United States is the only advanced economy in the world that does not guarantee paid vacation. It is also the only high-income country that does not require paid family and medical leave. And it's one of the only developed countries that still tie health care to employment, despite creating a national system."[3] We in this country are deluding ourselves that the most competitive economy is also the healthiest and the strongest. Nothing could be further from the truth.

Chantal Panozzo's husband accepted employment in Switzerland and she was concerned that she couldn't find a job in her career specialty. In the U.S. she had to work long hours, weekends and even some holidays and was discouraged from taking vacations. She needn't have worried. "My job title was the same, but I worked part time—and for a higher salary than I had received working full time in the United States. Not only that, but instead of two weeks of vacation, I had five. Once, when I went to Spain for 'only' 10 days, my Swiss colleagues chastised me for not going away long enough."[4]

If American business leaders think that pressuring employees to work longer hours often without additional compensation will produce a successful economy in the long run, perhaps they should redefine success. If the oligarchs are happy but their employees are not, that is the definition of a failed community. Chantal Panozzo worked shorter hours and fewer days doing the same thing in Switzerland as she had in the U.S. but something was different. "For the first time in my working life, I was living, too. Because of this my creativity flourished. I had both time and money, and because I had real time off, I was more productive when I was at work."[5]

In his book *Capital In 21st Century*, French economist Thomas Piketty warns that competition is producing economic inequality in the developed world "with potentially dire consequences for social justice and democratic governance."[6]

Competition can easily become a rationale for unbridled greed. Employers can engage in wage theft which is illegally paying workers less than minimum wage or not paying them overtime. "According to one multicity study, in a single week, nearly two-thirds of low-wage workers had, on average, 15 percent of their pay stolen by their employers."[7]

In a community where cooperation (and its cousin compassion) are valued, all members are accorded respect and are deemed worthy of support. Unfortunately in the U.S. an all too common but erroneous belief is that the poor are poor because they are lazy and unwilling to work and that the rich are willing to work harder or compete more intelligently.

We mentioned above that cooperation and compassion were related. Ironically, the poor, according to a 2009 McClatchy report have been shown to be more generous than the rich. Surprised? "Indeed, the U.S. Bureau of Labor Statistics' latest survey of consumer expenditure found that the poorest fifth of America's households contributed an average of 4.3 percent of their incomes to charitable organizations in 2007. The richest fifth gave at less than half that rate, 2.1 percent."[8]

Is it simply the nature of a human being to be fearful, greedy, self-centered and competitive? And if not, then when did this particular dimension of the false self-begin? Well, for at least a partial explanation, we can go back to the beginnings of modern civilization itself in both the East and the West. It will not surprise students of Simple Reality that our answer is contained in the worldview of these two disparate halves of the globe.

Richard E. Nisbett in his book *The Geography of Thought: How Asians and Westerners Think Differently ... and Why* begins to flesh out the distinctions between the worldviews of the Orient and the Occident. "As Nisbett shows through a wide range of studies and surveys, and observational research conducted by himself and his colleagues around the world, these two fundamentally different ways of conceiving and experiencing reality influence every aspect of our contemporary life—education, law, business, child-rearing, and social relations—and account for much of the misunderstanding about behavior and expectations that arise between Easterners and Westerners."[9]

Beginning 2,500 years ago in the *polis*, the Greek city-state, the highly competitive false-self identities ("me" or "I" as separate from the rest of humanity) made a bold entrance setting the stage for the drama of Western civilization. "A strong sense of individual identity accompanies the Greek sense of personal agency ... The history of Europe ... created a new sort of person—one who conceived of individuals as separate from the larger community and who thought in terms imbued with freedom."[10] To be accurate and with apologies to Mr. Nisbett, we must modify that last phrase to read "the *illusion* of freedom."

And now to the East. Our example will be China which had throughout its history a very homogeneous population. For example, even today 95 percent of the Chinese population belongs to the same Han ethnic group. "While the Greeks cherished *agency,* argued [competed] with each other in the marketplace, debated in the political assembly ... and thought of themselves 'as individuals with distinct properties, as units separate from others,' the Chinese embraced harmony as their social ideal [thanks to Confucius]. 'Every Chinese was first and foremost a member of a collective.'"[11] Of course harmony in a collective requires, you guessed it, cooperation, or what might be called "collective agency."

Not surprisingly, the teaching of Buddha was based on a worldview of Oneness which determines an identity for a practitioner who values cooperation. "For Easterners, close attention to relationships, attitudes, and the feelings of others gained in importance. Compromise and hostility resolution were highly valued."[12]

As we continue to experience the process of globalization within the human community, we will have the opportunity to shift the context containing competition to one where we can create more cooperation around the world. Neal Peirce writing in the Washington Post cites such an opportunity, "Because we are not partners in the European Union in order to *compete* but in order to *complete* another's work."[13] Cooperation is a healthy behavior and a unifying force among both individuals and nations. Sounds good, but as China struggles to create an economy that emulates a highly competitive capitalism, the ideals of Confucius, Lao Tse and Buddha may be replaced by the even older false-self survival strategy. There is ample evidence that the pursuit of plenty, pleasure and power is mesmerizing the people of China as competition becomes a more compelling behavior than cooperation.

We return to the West where self-destructive competition is more advanced. Unhealthy competition (and most competition in P-B is unhealthy) poisons self-expression, leads to a chain of reactions and often violence. "For example, as competition increases to get into top-ranked colleges, so does cheating among high school students. As sports become fiercer and more lucrative, injuries and doping rise even as careers shorten. And as meatpackers race to dominate global markets through lower prices, falling standards cause terrible cruelty, environmental degradation and dangerous, dead-end work."[14]

Seth has a more objective perspective than most of us caught up in P-B are able to attain. He makes the critical distinction between competition and violence. "In your society [America] and to some extent in others, the natural communication of aggression has broken down. You confuse violence with aggression, and do not understand aggression's creative activity or its purpose as a method of communication to *prevent* violence ... Violence is a distortion of aggression ... Any creative idea is aggressive. Violence is not aggressive. It is instead a passive surrender to emotion [a reaction] which is not understood or evaluated, only feared, and at the same time sought ... Both killer and victim in a war, for instance, are caught up in the same kind of passion, but the passion is not aggressive. It is its opposite—the desire for destruction."[15] In other words, violence is a "reaction" and as such an unsustainable behavior. "Know that yearning is made up of feelings of despair caused by a sense of powerlessness, not of power. Aggressiveness leads to action, to creativity and to life. It does not lead to destruction, violence or annihilation."[16] Without the presence of fear, the energy of the creative impulse in P-A is in harmony with the ever unfolding expression of Simple Reality.

The Great Irony

Hyde noted the irony of Ireland's copying the nation she most hated.
   Richard Kain

Many of the words we speak in P-B would have something approaching the opposite meaning in the context of P-A. Similarly, a playwright will use irony having characters delivering lines that have a profound meaning but to which they (the actor's character) are oblivious but that the audience understands. The greatest irony in the human community is the incongruity between illusion and reality, between what seems to be happening and what is actually happening. In meditation we gain the perspective of a theatre audience or that of our True self and can observe the irony or incongruity between a reaction and a response and thereby are empowered to respond more profoundly to life.

The majority of the people in the global village are like the actors on stage who in the context of the play are acting and speaking in a rational way. However, from the perspective of the objective observer, free from the beliefs, attitudes and values of the deluded false self, the self-destructive behavior is obvious. We are all contained in a perfect Creation, the Kingdom of Heaven within, but we are mesmerized by and use our energy to choose and create a narrative that is a "Hell" of suffering and pain. Ironic, don't you think?

When a lion wants to kill large prey such as a zebra it suffocates it by closing off the air passage by gripping the throat or by taking the entire nose into its mouth and blocking the flow of air. The false self is cutting off the flow of awareness in the human species, depriving homo-sapiens of the choice of a sustainable community. Irony enters in when we realize that we continue to choose a survival strategy that is killing us. We choose to remain unconscious distracting ourselves from or denying the existence of Simple Reality. We have a choice to breath in the life-enhancing joy of the present moment. Let's find the courage to get the lion off our back before he has us by the throat.

Integration and Disintegration

One of the possible meanings of the word integration is to make whole. Disintegration, on the other hand, is to cause a whole to separate into its component parts or to cause the destruction of that whole. We have learned that P-B is a shattered whole which is self-destructing. Simple Reality is a narrative that will make whole again that which is disintegrating.

The jig-saw puzzle makes a good analogy for this process of disintegration. The dis-assembled puzzle (P-B) is "disintegrated". It makes no sense. It is a chaotic, disassociated jumble, an illusion of seemingly related pieces.

A strategy or process of assembling the puzzle (the Point of Power Practice) will integrate the puzzle pieces into a meaningful whole (P-A) as one's life becomes a focused meditation of continually choosing response over reaction. Each piece or each successful moment spent in the Now is naturally related to every other such experience and these moments begin to cluster into larger and larger or longer and longer moments. A pattern begins to emerge, life begins to become a healthier and more meaningful story and our new identity begins to come into focus.

As each individual begins to see the meaning in his individual "puzzle" a larger pattern emerges wherein the individual puzzles begin to merge into a global pattern, an integrated global village. And finally, just as a symphony is born out of the integration of each instrument into a harmonious expression, the puzzle that is the entirety of Creation comes into focus, perfectly integrated into a compassionate, beautiful expression of Oneness.

Sometimes integration need involve nothing more than recognizing the non-existent illusion of formerly held beliefs and transcending those, letting them go. For example, the word and concept of "race" has been behind a lot of self-destructive human behavior—doubly sad, because there is no such thing as race. Yale University biologist Jonathan Marks puts it succinctly. "Race has no basic biological reality. The human species simply doesn't come packaged that way."¹

Like much of P-B, if we believe something, it is "real" to us, making it of paramount importance that we distinguish illusion from reality, appearances from substance. It seems that humanity has "made-up" the mental construct of "race." Robert Boyd zeroes in on the origin of the illusion of race: "A majority of biologists and anthropologists drawing on a growing body of evidence accumulated since the 1970's, have concluded that race is a social, cultural and political concept based largely on superficial appearance."²

In other words the idea of race, like all of the attitudes, beliefs and values contained in P-B, was created by the fear-driven human mind. Many of us will make the association between the illusion of "race" and another disastrous illusion called the "*other*." In this way we begin to piece together the chaotic puzzle of human suffering.

If race is not a sufficient reason to defend the illusion of the "*other*" then how about religion? No religious group has resisted integration into the wider human community more vociferously than the Jews. "Only through this full obedience [to the Torah], they felt, could the Jews escape assimilation and extinction."³ The previous statement refers to the Jewish struggle during Roman dominance in Judea. "After the Temple was destroyed (A.D. 70), the priesthood lost influence, the Sadducees disappeared, the synagogue replaced the temple, and the Pharisees, through the rabbis, became the teachers and shepherds of a scattered but undefeated people."⁴

The principle of Oneness calls for the integration of the world's peoples and gives the lie to perceived differences of any kind including the illusion of religious differences. Two thousand years after the Jews were driven from Judea by the Romans, anti-semitism remains a problem for Jews around the world. And yet who can blame any people who are loath to integrate into the unhealthy and self-destructive behaviors of the majority P-B culture? And yet, that's what has to happen. Religion, race, the *other* and all similar elements of the disintegrating human community must be integrated and/or transcended.

Our reactions are like pieces of a puzzle that need to be integrated or put together. Some of the reactions originate from our past conditioning; others are repressed elements of our shadow, experiences too painful to consciously acknowledge at the time. Each time we respond to emerging shadow material we are constructing a stronger True self and dismantling the false self. "Integration of the shadow is always concurrent with the dissolution of the false persona."[5]

Integration and disintegration are at the heart of creating a new identity by shifting paradigms. This process, the highest human attainment has, as we might expect, incredible rewards. Marsha Sinetar describes those rewards, "The individual feels subjectively safe. He is emotionally connected and experiences no separation, no splitting or fragmentation. He doesn't *feel* isolated, separate or alone because—in a real way—his is connected, bonded, safe, 'at-one-with,' at home."[6]

There is more than one way to language the process and experience of assembling a puzzle. John Ruskan, the author of *Emotional Clearing* describes the process from his perspective. "[Experience] must be digested in a certain way, called *direct experience*, in which it is absorbed or dissolved completely. The ability for direct experience is gained through the cultivation of 'being in the moment.' Being in the moment is a mystical perspective. *Witness consciousness* is activated, and we function on a new and higher plane that results in a sense of well-being and euphoria as well as calling into play transpersonal powers that have been blocked by the personal ego. These powers operate on a very practical level, effecting *transformation* in situations that we previously resisted. By accepting, we go beyond. We reach the spiritual through the mundane. We discover the spiritual *in* the mundane."[7] The mundane Ruskan refers to is the energy contained in a potential reaction that can be transformed into awareness by responding.

Ruskan calls his process of responding Integrative Processing. "Integration brings freedom from pain. Integration does not mean that the negative side of any dualistic experience is eliminated, but that our perception of the negative changes so it is no longer disturbing ... We find ourselves with a new awareness and freedom; we have grown; happiness is unconditional."[8]

The Steps of Integrative Processing

	Step	Plane	Function
1.	Awareness	Intellectual	Knowing
2.	Acceptance	Mental	Thinking
3.	Direct Experience	Body	Feeling
4.	Transformation	Spiritual	Transcending[9]

Each one of us has at birth not only the desire to restore wholeness to our experience but the innate wisdom to accomplish this most glorious of human expressions. Without a new, wholesome and healthy narrative to provide a context for the integration of all of the world's peoples, antagonistic and divisive conflicts will prevail around the world and they will be based on religious, cultural, ethnic and other differences that have no basis in reality. Unless humanity can awaken to the truth of Simple Reality then mutual self-destruction will continue to be a dominant storyline with an ending too horrible to contemplate.

Values

A value is a principle, standard, or quality considered worthwhile or desirable.

> *It is essential that the student acquire an understanding of and lively feeling for values. He must acquire a vivid sense of the beautiful and of the morally good. Otherwise he, with his specialized knowledge more closely resembles a well-trained dog than a harmoniously developed person.*
> Albert Einstein

We can evaluate the relative health of a community by whether its beliefs, attitudes and values are life affirming. Taking more than one measurement over time may also indicate in which direction a community's values may be trending, that is to say, toward increasing sickness or toward awakening and healing. The following behaviors unfortunately are not a cause for optimism.

Oh! If I could just become a legend in my own time.

Columnist Petula Dvorak asks the pertinent question: "What do you think kids want most in life today? Money? Marriage? Adventure? A cool job? Spiritual fulfillment? Nope."[1] Generation Y according to a study by psychology professors at UCLA, rank "fame" as the number one value. We can assume they mean more than the "15 minute" duration allotted to the rest of us. This is something of a recent shift.

In 1997 the top 5 values among the young were community feeling, benevolence (being kind and helping others), image, tradition and self-acceptance. We would consider those to be good values, do you agree? And what's encouraging is that compassion was inherent in those values.

In 2007, a similar study by UCLA, found that the top five values emphasized in television shows popular with children were fame, achievement, popularity, image and financial success.

Studies like those at UCLA give us a snapshot in time of an evolving P-B narrative. The list, therefore, will always indicate predominantly unhealthy choices. "In 2007, benevolence dropped to the 12th spot and community feeling fell to the 11th."[2]

Nevertheless, the following behaviors are alarming even in a nation as dysfunctional and neurotic as the United States. How do young high schoolers go about becoming famous? In Northern Virginia at least, they do it by producing and distributing teen porn. Three teenage boys made sex videos with six teenage girls from their own school and two neighboring high schools.

Even though the three boys were locked up and face the serious charge of possession and distribution of child pornography, there are some who think they have achieved that all-important goal. A commenter on the website "Jesus Phreak" wrote that the three boys' bad behavior was, "Pretty epic. These kids will be legendary at West Springfield for years to come."[3] Who could possibly want more than that?

Appendix -
The Point of Power Practice

Taking Complete Control of Your Choices

We don't have to be highly intelligent to understand Simple Reality because it is indeed simple. We don't have to be highly disciplined spiritual ascetics, withdrawing from normal life to practice constant contemplation or meditation, waiting decades for transcendence. Simple Reality is not complex or impossibly difficult and we experience the benefits immediately. The caveat here is that we do have to be awake, focused and motivated. Remember that we want our life to become an intentional meditation every moment of every day. The Point of Power Practice as the central focus of that meditation will provide us with the authentic power and positive use of energy to be successful.

He that is slow to anger is better than the mighty;
and he that ruleth his spirit than he that taketh a city.
    Proverbs 16:32

The goal of the Point of Power Practice involves choosing to respond rather than react every moment of every day. Each time this is accomplished, we find ourselves experiencing Simple Reality. Because the goal of meditation when profoundly understood is experiencing Reality as it really is, we can say that in using this practice our life becomes a meditation.

When our past false-self survival strategy or other conditioning is triggered, that moment is the "point of power." At that "point" we are presented with an all-important choice. We are stuck in P-B when we choose to react, to identify with the body, mind or emotions. What inevitably follows is the experience of afflictive emotions and suffering. If we pause, remain calm and breathe, choosing to respond, we will experience the "feeling" that characterizes P-A or Simple Reality. The breath is the "thread" that leads through the heart to the present moment and thus to the Implicate Order, which is the source of the wisdom and energy that connects all of Creation.

To hear the same process described in a variety of ways might help internalize the meaning at a deeper level. For example, in choosing response over reaction one is able, as Marcus Aurelius said, "to give the preference to the good thing … and freely choose the better, and hold to it."[1]

We contrast the description above by a Roman Emperor/philosopher with the modern language of psychology. "The beginner learns to identify harmful behavior," says Daniel Brown, "and then 'practice the opposite' behavior … According to the laws of cause and effect such opponent action will manifest as positive changes in the stream of consciousness over time; behavior change contributes to intra-psychic change."[2] In other words we will have begun the process of shifting paradigms and acquiring a new identity. What follows is the new behavior of a compassionate, liberated person.

The whole strategy of the Point of Power Practice is to remain present while in the context of Simple Reality. Seth says "you can change your experience by altering your beliefs about yourself and physical existence … we create our personal reality through our conscious beliefs about ourselves, others, and the world. Following this is the concept that the 'point of power' is in the present, not in the past of this life or any other."[3]

"You get what you concentrate upon."[4] The Point of Power Practice, choosing response over reaction, ensures that we are concentrating on a wholesome and sustainable narrative, something inherently "Real."

Human suffering includes craving for plenty, pleasure and power. We all know the illusory nature of obtaining material wealth and feeling empty, of experiencing pleasure and still wanting more, and having others within our power and control and still feeling helpless. The Point of Power Practice, choosing response over reaction, delivers authentic power, the power of choosing a sustainable story, a wholesome identity and compassionate behavior.

And finally to Ken Wilber who expresses himself in a fascinating, although somewhat, what can I say, "Wilberian" language. As a master synthesizer he is one of the few people who can give us both an Eastern and Western perspective. He says that in "Buddhist traditions the primordial state is one of immediacy ... The meditator must learn to negate the more common forms of reactivity—expectations, doubts, evaluatory thought, and the incessant attempt to categorize the unfolding experience. Consciousness as we ordinarily know it in the West is not pure awareness but rather awareness as it is embodied in the psychological structure of the mind or the brain ... These two components, awareness and psychological structure, constitute a gestalt, an overall interacting, dynamic system that makes up consciousness. Techniques exist, however, that are intended to free a person's awareness from the dominance of the structure, of the machinery that has been programmed into him."[5]

Such a technique is the Point of Power Practice. Use it! You'll be glad you did.

What the heck is the Point of Power Practice?

The **POINT OF POWER PRACTICE** is choosing **RESPONSE OVER REACTION**, authentic power, a sustainable story, a wholesome identity and compassionate behavior.

 FALSE SELF   **TS** **TRUE SELF**

REACT
PARADIGM-B

 - OR -

RESPOND
PARADIGM-A

When our mind is triggered by our false self (**FS**) or other conditioning, we choose to identify with our body, mind and emotions. This causes suffering for us and others.

Choosing to pause, remain calm and breathe, we experience our false self (**FS**) losing its grip on our body, mind and emotions. This creates space for the true self (**TS**) to be in the present moment. You and others are no longer suffering.

Our breath is also affected by the triggers, it becomes shallow as we experience a fight or flight reaction. We are no longer in the present moment which causes suffering for us and others.

By focusing on the breath (responding) we choose the present moment, the true self (**TS**), the heart, which is the source of wisdom, energy and Oneness.

"Fear is the excitement without the breath."
FRITZ PERLS

The next time you are triggered remember this:

Stimulus + Response = Serenity

Notes

Chapter 1 – The Human Community: Where We Have Been
Introduction
1. Hutchins, Robert Maynard [ed.]. *The Great Ideas: A Syntopicon of Great Books of the Western World Vol. II*. Chicago: Encyclopedia Britannica, Inc. 1952, 437.
2. Henry, Roy Charles. "Time." *Science & Philosophy: The Failure of Reason in the Human Community*. My Simple Reality, 2015, 242.
3. Durant, Will and Ariel Durant. *The Age of Voltaire*. New York: Simon and Schuster, 1965, 709.
4. Durant, Will. *Caesar and Christ*. New York: Simon and Schuster, 1944, 95.
5. Ibid.
6. Durant, Will and Ariel Durant. *Rousseau and Revolution*. New York: Simon and Schuster, 1967, 709.
7. *Ibid.*, 794.
8. *Ibid.*, 808.
9. *Ibid.*, 807.

The Evolution of American Identity
1. Davidson, Marshall B. *The American Heritage History of The Writers' America*. New York: American Heritage, 1973, 15.
2. *Ibid.*, 17.
3. *Ibid.*, 18.
4. *Ibid.*, 28.
5. *Ibid.*, 32.
6. *Ibid.*
7. *Ibid.*, 50.
8. Chang, Kenneth. "Sacvan Bercovitch, 81; Traced Oratory to Puritans." *The New York Times*. January 8, 2015, B11.
9. Davidson, *op. cit.*, 67.
10. *Ibid.*
11. *Ibid.*, 87.
12. *Ibid.*, 95.
13. *Ibid.*, 89.
14. Strayed, Cheryl. "Bookends." *The New York Times Book Review*. January 18, 2015, 27.
15. Davidson, *op. cit.*, 104.
16. *Ibid.*, 121.
17. *Ibid.*, 132.
18. *Ibid.*
19. *Ibid.*, 123.
20. *Ibid.*
21. *Ibid.*, 266.

22 *Ibid.*, 149.
23 *Ibid.*
24 *Ibid.*, 152.
25 *Ibid.*, 154.
26 *Ibid.*, 238.
27 *Ibid.*, 247.
28 *Ibid.*, 266.
29 *Ibid.*
30 *Ibid.*, 294.
31 *Ibid.*, 268.
32 *Ibid.*, 268-269.
33 *Ibid.*, 272.
34 *Ibid.*, 243.
35 *Ibid.*, 270.
36 *Ibid.*, 276.
37 *Ibid.*, 289.
38 *Ibid.*, 291.
39 *Ibid.*
40 *Ibid.*, 337.
41 *Ibid.*
42 *Ibid.*, 345.
43 *Ibid.*, 377.
44 Bass, Holly. "How It Feels to Be Black in America." *The New York Times Book Review*. December 28, 2014, 9.
45 Kirsch, Adam. "Bookends." *The New York Times Book Review*. January 18, 2015, 27.
46 Williams, John. "Open Book." *The New York Times Book Review*. December 28, 2014, 4.

Beware! The Nerds Are Ascendant: Bill Gates Is On The Move
1 Henry, Roy Charles. *Science & Philosophy: The Failure of Reason in the Human Community*. My Simple Reality, 2015.
2 Sorkin, Andrew Ross. "Everything is Illuminated." *The New York Times Magazine*. September 7, 2014, 32.
3 "The Great Courses" [advertisement]. *The New York Times*. September 7, 2014.
4 Yogananda, Paramahansa. *Autobiography of a Yogi*. Los Angeles. Self-Realization Fellowship, 1946, 151.
5 Shankara. *The Crest-Jewel of Discrimination*. New York: New American Library, 1947, 18.
6 Durant, Will and Ariel Durant. *Rousseau and Revolution*. New York: Simon and Schuster, 1967, 431.
7 St. John of the Cross. *Ascent of Mount Carmel*. Liguori Missouri: Triumph Books, 1991, 222.
8 Tolstoy, Leo. *A Calendar of Wisdom*. New York: Scribner, 1997, 185.
9 Pagels, Elaine. *The Origin of Satan*. New York. Random House, 1995, 167.

10. *Ibid.*
11. Magill, Frank N. ed. *Masterpieces of World Literature*. New York: Harper, 1989, 254.
12. Durant, Will. *Our Oriental Heritage*. New York: Simon and Schuster, 1954, 916.
13. *Ibid.*, 964.
14. "Bill Gates's Big Idea For A History Class." *The New York Times*. September 21, 2014, 14.

The Illusion of Change
1. Alter, Adam. "Where We Are Shapes Who We Are." *The New York Times Sunday Review*. June 16, 2013, 12.
2. *Ibid.*
3. *Ibid.*
4. *Ibid.*
5. Sankaran, Lavanya. "Caste Is Not Past." *The New York Times Sunday Review*. June 16, 2013, 9.
6. *Ibid.*

Crossroads
1. Durant, Will. *Our Oriental Heritage*. New York: Simon and Schuster, 1954, 651.
2. *Ibid.*, 656.
3. *Ibid.*, 674-675.
4. *Ibid.*, 676.
5. *Ibid.*
6. Tierney, John. "A Meditation on the Art of Not Trying." *The New York Times*. December 16, 2014, D8.
7. *Ibid.*
8. Williams, John. "Open Book." *The New York Times Book Review*. December 21, 2014, 4.
9. Csikszentmihalyi, Mihaly. *Flow: The Psychology of Optimal Experience*. New York: Harper Collins, July 1, 2008, 212.
10. Davidson, Marshall B. *The American Heritage History of The Writers' America*. New York: American Heritage, 1973, 171.
11. Feiler, Bruce. "The New Allure of Sacred Pilgrimages." *The New York Times*. December 21, 2014, 7.
12. *Ibid.*
13. Worthen Molly. "The Franciscan Age." *The New York Times Book Review*. December 21, 2014, 15.
14. Brooks, David. "The Subtle Sensation Of Faith." *The New York Times*. December 23, 2014, A25.

History, Time and Progress
1. Hutchins, Robert Maynard [ed.], *Great Books of the Western World: The Great Ideas: A Syntopicon Vol. II*. Encyclopedia Britannica, Inc. 1952, 437.
2. Rampell Catherine. "The Half-Trillion-Dollar Depression." *The New York Times Magazine*. July 7, 2013, 14.

3. *Ibid.*
4. *AARP Bulletin: Real Possibilities.* July/August 2013, 6.
5. Hutchins, *op. cit.*, 439.
6. *Ibid.*
7. *Ibid.*, 628.
8. *Ibid.*, 441.
9. *Ibid.*, 443.

A Brave Stupidity
1. Durant, Will. *Our Oriental Heritage.* New York: Simon and Schuster, 1954, viii.
2. *Ibid.*, 21.
3. *Ibid.*, 68.
4. *Ibid.*, 71.
5. *Ibid.*, 99.
6. *Ibid.*, 120.
7. *Ibid.*, 285.
8. *Ibid.*, 140.
9. Aurelius, Marcus. *The Meditations of Marcus Aurelius.* New York: Avon, 1993, 19.
10. Durant, *op. cit.*, 141.
11. *Ibid.*, 205.
12. *Ibid.*, 347.
13. *Ibid.*, 348.

Solomon the Schmuck
1. Durant, Will. *Our Oriental Heritage.* New York: Simon and Schuster, 1954, 306.
2. *Ibid.*, 306-308.
3. *Ibid.*, 308.
4. *Ibid.*
5. *Ibid.*, 307.

Power In Persia
1. Durant, Will. *Our Oriental Heritage.* New York: Simon and Schuster, 1954, pp. 367-371.
2. *Ibid.*
3. *Ibid.*

Jerusalem Day: Triumph or Disaster
1. Rudoren, Jodi. "Forged in Battle." *The New York Times Book Review.* November 20, 2013, 20.
2. *Ibid.*

Doomed by Darwin in P-B
1. Durant, Will. *Our Oriental Heritage.* New York: Simon and Schuster, 1954, p. 928.
2. *Ibid.*

In Search of P-A
1. Durant, Will. *The Life of Greece.* New York: Simon and Schuster, 1939, 141.

2 *Ibid.*, 175.
3 *Ibid.*, 242.
4 *Ibid.*, 262.
5 *Ibid.*, 578.
6 *Ibid.*, 667.
7 *Ibid.*
8 *Ibid.*

The Writing Is On The Wall
1 Durant, Will. *Caesar and Christ*. New York: Simon and Schuster, 1944, 79.
2 *Ibid.*, 88.
3 *Ibid.*
4 *Ibid.*, 132-133.
5 "Aspen home prices gain, now highest in nation." *The Denver Post*. March 5, 2011, 6B.
6 Lofholm, Nancy. "A Lift from the depths." *The Denver Post*. November 20, 2014, 1A.
7 Durant, op. cit., 89.
8 *Ibid.*, 88-89.
9 *Ibid.*, 81.
10 *Ibid.*, 90.
11 *Ibid.*
12 *Ibid.*, 90-91.
13 *Ibid.*, 142.
14 *Ibid.*
15 *Ibid.*, 143.
16 *Ibid.*, 81.

Lost On The Ocean Blue
1 Jaffe, Adrian H. and Virgil Scott. *Studies in the Short Story*. New York: Holt, 1968, 2-3.
2 Walt, Stephen M. "American exceptionalism?" *The Denver Post*. October 16, 2011, 5D.
3 *Ibid.*
4 Danner, Mark. "No Exit." *The New York Times Sunday Review*. February 1, 2015, 1.
5 Walt, *op. cit.*
6 *Ibid.*
7 Campbell, Joseph. *The Power of Myth*. New York: Bantam, 1988, xv.

Ghosts
1 Pogash, Carol. "To Some Indians in California, Missions Founder Is Far From a Saint." *The New York Times*. January 22, 2015, A12.
2 *Ibid.*, A15.
3 *The Denver Post*. "Crime hits Indians hardest." February 15, 1999, 1A.
4 Carman, Diane. "Even today, Sand Creek's bloody reality is hard to face." *The Denver Post*. August 4, 2005, 5B.
5 *Ibid.*

6 *Ibid.*
7 Egan, Timothy. "Tribes sue government over oil mismanagement." *The Denver Post.* March 11, 1999, 1A and 24A.
8 *Ibid.*, 24A.
9 Blinder, Alan. "150 Years Later, Wrestling With a Revised View of Sherman's March." *The New York Times.* November 15, 2014, A9.
10 *Ibid.*
11 *Ibid.*
12 *Ibid.*, A15.
13 *Ibid.*
14 Lewis, David Levering. "The Segregated North." *The New York Times Book Review.* January 11, 2015, 13.
15 Gonnerman, Jennifer. "Brutal Territory." *The New York Times Book Review.* January 25, 2015, 1.
16 *Ibid.*, 20.
17 Goldhagen, Daniel Johah. "How Auschwitz Is Misunderstood." *The New York Times.* January 25, 2015, 3.
18 *Ibid.*
19 Lyman, Rick. "For Auschwitz Museum, A Time of Great Change." *The New York Times.* January 24, 2015, A8.
20 Goldhagen, *op. cit.*

The Mirrors of History
1 LeBor, Adam. "Overt and Covert." *The New York Times Book Review.* November 10, 2013, 50.
2 *Ibid.*
3 *Ibid.*
4 Mazzetti, Mark. "C.I.A. Report Found Value of Brutal Interrogation Was Inflated." *The New York Times.* January 21, 2015, A7.
5 Frum, David. "Who Decided?" *The New York Times Book Review.* October 20, 2013, 12.
6 *Ibid.*
7 Rojas, Rick. "Parcel for Sale: A Lot of Space. Light? Well …" *The New York Times.* January 15, 2015, A18.

History: A Story, Your Story, Our Story and *The* Story
1 Wissler, Clark, et. al. *The Pageant of America: Adventures in the Wilderness.* New Haven: Yale University Press, 1925, 183.
2 Sokolove, Michael. "Down By Law." *The New York Times Magazine.* November 9, 2014, 46.
3 *Ibid.*
4 *Denver Post, The.* "Heat-Not-Burn Cigarette On Way." November 18, 2014, 8A.
5 *Ibid.*
6 Seelye, Katharine Q. "In Anti-Smoke Town, Firestorm." *The New York Times.* November 18, 2014, A1.
7 *Ibid.*, A16.
8 *Ibid.*

9. Davenport, Coral. "In Climate Deal, Obama May Set A Theme For 2016." November 13, 2014, A1.
10. *Ibid.*
11. Kristof, Nicholas. "When Whites Just Don't Get It, Part 4." *The New York Times Sunday Review.* November 16, 2014, 9.
12. *Ibid.*
13. *The New York Times.* "Millions Forced to Live as Slaves, A Human Rights Group Reports." November 18, 2014, A6.
14. Durant, Will and Ariel Durant. *Rousseau and Revolution.* New York: Simon and Schuster, 1967, 940.

History: His-story And Her-story

1. Bennhold, Katrin. "Forget the Hounds. As Foxes Creep In, Britons Call the Sniper." *The New York Times.* December 7, 2014, 12.
2. Collins, Gail. "The Woes Of Working Women." *The New York Times.* December 6, 2014, A21.
3. Stensrud, Jessica. "Letters." *The New York Times.* December 7, 2014, 6.
4. *New York Times, The.* "Women Who Work." December 1, 2014.
5. Bennhold, Katrin. "Major Gain For Women In Church of England." *The New York Times.* November 18, 2014, A4.
6. *Ibid.*
7. Gladstone, Rick. "U.N. Report Shows an Increase in Trafficking Children." *The New York Times.* November 25, 2014, A10.
8. Eltahawy, Mona. "Fighting Female Genital Mutilation." *The New York Times.* November 17, 2014, A23.
9. *Ibid.*
10. *Ibid.*
11. *Ibid.*
12. Kristof, Nicholas. "Politicians, Teens and Birth Control." *The New York Times.* November 13, 2014.owen, Annie. "Deaths put spotlight on India sterilization camps." *The Denver Post.* November 14, 2014, A27.
13. *Ibid.*
14. *Ibid.*
15. Gowen, Annie. "Deaths put spotlight on India sterilization camps." *The Denver Post.* November 14, 2014, 20A.
16. *Ibid.*
17. Barry, Ellen and Suhasini Raj. "Web of Incentives in Fatal Indian Sterilizations." *The New York Times.* November 13, 2014, A16.
18. *The New York Times.* "India's Lethal Approach to Birth Control." November 21, 2014, A26.
19. Steinhauer, Jennifer. "Widening Spotlight On Assault Of Women." *The New York Times.* December 5, 2014, A13.
20. *Ibid.*
21. *Ibid.*, A20.
22. Steinhauer, Jennifer, and Richard Perez-Pena. "Leadership Of University Vows to Act Against Rape." *The New York Times.* November 26, 2014, A21.

23 *Ibid.*, A19.
24 *Ibid.*, A29.
25 *Ibid.*
26 Draper, Robert. "In The Company Of Men." *The New York Times Magazine.* November 30, 2014, 31.
27 Irwin, Neil. "With Aid, More People Work." *The New York Times.* December 18, 2014, B1.
28 *Ibid.*, B8.

Chapter 2 – The Human Community: Where We Are Now
Introduction
1 Wolfers, Justin. "How Economists Came to Dominate the Conversation." *The New York Times.* January 27, 2015, A3.

The Ostrich
1 Keillor, Garrison. "George W. Bush is a small 'p' president." *Rocky Mountain News.* February 11, 2006, 10C.
2 Samuelson, Robert J. "Specter of economic instability haunts globe." *Rocky Mountain News.* March 19, 2005, 12C.
3 Goodman, Ellen. "Betty Friedan really did change U.S. women's lives." *The Rocky Mountain News.* February 11, 2006, 11C.
4 Brown, Jennifer. "Mental Illnesses rise on college campuses." *The Denver Post.* April 3, 2006, 1A.
5 Rodriguez, Cindy. "Recycling words into weapons." *The Denver Post.* March 14, 2006, 1F.
6 Pitts, Leonard. "The things we did for love." *The Denver Post.* February 16, 2005, 7B.
7 Eckholm, Eric. "Black men's plight worse than believed." *The Denver Post.* March 20, 2006, 2A.
8 Pozner, Larry. "Gambling is state's two-faced coin." *The Denver Post.* March 12, 2006, 3E.
9 Harrop Froma. "More common sense in war on drugs." *The Denver Post.* December 30, 2010, 5E.

Crazy Metaphors? Maybe Not!
1 Ronson, Jon. "Feelings?" *The New York Times Book Review.* June 16, 2013, 12.
2 *Ibid.*
3 Kahneman, Daniel. *Thinking, Fast and Slow.* New York: Farrar, 2011, 27-28.
4 Worth, Robert F. "Mad Bombers." *The New York Times Magazine.* June 16, 2013, 46.
5 *Ibid.*
6 *Ibid.*, 47.
7 Byers, Sam. "The Smart Smoker." *The New York Times Magazine.* June 16, 2013, 52.
8 *Ibid.*

He's Onto Something!
1   Brodesser-Akner, Taffy. "I Can't Think Of Anything Less Funny Than Dying In A Zombie Attack." *The New York Times Magazine*. June 23, 2013, 20-21.
2   *Ibid.*
3   *Ibid.*
4   *Ibid.*

Bad Choices
1   Durant, Will. *The Reformation*. New York: Simon and Schuster, 1957, 3.
2   *Ibid.*
3   *Ibid.*, 4.
4   *Ibid.*, 18.
5   *Ibid.*, 25.
6   Goodstein, Laurie. "Some Mormons Search the Web and Find Doubt." *The New York Times Sunday Review*. July 21, 2013, 4.
7   *Ibid.*
8   *Ibid.*
9   *Ibid.*
10 *Ibid.*

The Decline And Fall Of Practically Everybody
1   Singer, Jeffrey. "The Gambling Palace as a Lifeline." *The New York Times Sunday Review*. August 25, 2013, 23.
2   *Ibid.*
3   *Ibid.*

Feeding Frenzy: The Return Of The Stocks
1   Ronson, Jon. "Feed Frenzy." *The New York Times Magazine*. February 15, 2015, 24.
2   *Ibid.*, 25.
3   Carrigan William D. and Clive Webb. "When Americans Lynched Mexicans." *The New York Times*. February 20, 2015, A23.
4   Barnard, Anne. "Children, Caged for Effect, To Mimic Imagery of ISIS." *The New York Times*. February 21, 2015, A9.
5   *Ibid.*
6   *Ibid.*
7   Ronson, *op. cit.*, 22.
8   *Ibid.*
9   *Ibid.*, 25.
10 Kantor, Jodi. "Lawsuits' Lurid Details Draw an Online Crowd." *The New York Times*. February 23, 2015, A3.
11 *Ibid.*

Discouraging Compassion
1   Kolker, Robert. "Attention Must Be Paid." *The New York Times Book Review*. September 28, 2014, 12.
2   *Ibid.*
3   *Ibid.*
4   *Ibid.*

Euphoria Or Dysphoria: Virtual Delusion
1. Heffernan, Virginia. "Seeing Is Believing." *The New York Times Magazine.* November 16, 2014, 54.
2. *Ibid.*
3. *Ibid.*, 56.
4. *Ibid.*
5. *Ibid.*, 57.
6. *Ibid.*
7. Heffernan, *op. cit.*

Happiness Is Pursuit Of Security, Sensation And Power—Not!
1. Luhrmann, T.M. "The Anxious American." *The New York Times.* July 19, 2015, 9.
2. Cederstrom, Carl. "The Dangers of Happiness." *The New York Times.* July 19, 2015, 8.
3. *Ibid.*
4. Easterbrook, Gregg. "The Real Truth About Money." *TIME.* January 17, 2005, A32.
5. *Ibid.*
6. *Ibid.*, A33.
7. *Ibid.*
8. Vlahos, James. "Money Game." *The New York Times Magazine.* February 2, 2014, 28.
9. *Ibid.*, 29.
10. Douthat, Ross "Pot And Jackpots." *The New York Times Sunday Review* November 3, 2013, 12.
11. *Ibid.*
12. Whitehead, Barbara Dafoe. "Gaming the Poor." *The New York Times Sunday Review.* June 22, 2014, 7.
13. *Ibid.*
14. *Ibid.*
15. *Ibid.*
16. Douthat, *op. cit.*
17. Harrop, Froma. "Common sense vs. drug war." *The Denver Post.* November 28, 2006, 7B.
18. Douthat, *op. cit.*
19. Harrop, *op. cit.*
20. *Ibid.*
21. *Ibid.*
22. Associated Press, The. "Global Obesity Costs Skyrocket." *The Denver Post.* November 21, 2014, 15A.
23. Paul, Pamela. "The Power to Uplift." *TIME.* January 17, 2005, A45.
24. Bruni, Frank. "Lost in America." *The New York Times.* August 26, 2014, A23.

War Weary?
1. Brooks, Rosa. "A Call to Rally." *The New York Times Book Review.* June 29, 2015, 21.

2. *Ibid.*
3. Roy Charles Henry. "War Table." *Why Am I Here? The Third Great Question Concerning the Nature of Reality.* October 2014, 472-473.
4. Bronner, Ethan. "A Damaging Distance." *The New York Times Book Review.* July 13, 2014, 3.
5. *Ibid.*
6. Schroeder, Juliana. "Peace Through Friendship." *The New York Times Book Review.* August 24, 2014, 7.
7. Filkins, Dexter. "Knife Fights." *The New York Times Book Review.* November 16, 2014, 21.
8. Foden, Giles. "Everything Has Its Price." *The New York Times Book Review.* February 22, 2015, 20.
9. *Ibid.*
10. *Ibid.*
11. Bissell, Tom. "A War With No Sides." *The New York Times Book Review.* March 1, 2015ercy, Jennifer. "The Wake of Grief." *The New York Times Book Review.* February 22, 2015, 13.
12. Percy, Jennifer. "The Wake of Grief." *The New York Times Book Review.* February 22, 2015, 18.
13. *Ibid.*
14. *Ibid.*
15. Rohde, David. "The Invisible Front." *The New York Times Book Review.* November 16, 2014, 22.

We Can Do This
1. Davidson, Marshall B. *The American Heritage History of The Writers' America.* New York: American Heritage, 1973, 384.
2. *Ibid.*
3. *Ibid.*
4. Larrabee, Eric. *Horizon.* January 1960, 10.

Response or Reaction: Marshmallows, One or Two
1. Bourne, Michael. "We Didn't Eat the Marshmallow. The Marshmallow Ate Us." *The New York Times Magazine.* January 12, 2014, 44.
2. Goleman, Daniel. *Emotional Intelligence.* New York: Bantam, 1995, 81-82.
3. *Ibid.*
4. *Ibid.*

Choosing Compassion
1. Balk, Meredith. "Ironically, For Children." *The New York Times.* July 26, 2015, 8.
2. Kristof, Nicholas. "A Millennial Named Bush." *The New York Times.* July 26, 2015, 9.
3. *Ibid.*

For Love or Money
1. Pollan, Michael. "The Trip Treatment." *The New York Times Magazine.* February 9, 2015, 47.
2. *Ibid.*

3   Heard, Gerald. "Can This Drug Enlarge Man's Mind." *Horizon*. May 1963, 29.
4   *Ibid.*, 31.
5   *Ibid.*, 114.
6   Pollan, *op. cit.*, 39.
7   *Ibid.*, 38.
8   *Ibid.*, 40.
9   *Ibid.*
10 *Ibid.*, 42.
11 *Ibid.*, 43.

Religion or No Religion? That Is the Question. Whether Tis Nobler … Blah, Blah, Blah …
1   Ross, Nancy Wilson. "The Square Roots of Zen." *Horizon*. July 1959, 73.
2   *Ibid.*, 71.
3   *Ibid.*
4   *Ibid.*, 72.
5   *Ibid.*, 73.
6   *Ibid.*
7   *Ibid.*
8   *Ibid.*, 75.

Chapter 3: The Future of the Human Community
The Robotic False Self
1   Menaker, Daniel. "Our Tools, Ourselves." *The New York Times Book Review*. November 9, 2014, 11.
2   Murphy, Kate. "No Time to Think." *The New York Times*. July 27, 2014, 3.
3   *Ibid.*
4   *Ibid.*
5   Franzen, Jonathan. "Left to Our Own Devices." *The New York Times Book Review*. October 4, 2015, 1.
6   *Ibid.*, 22.
7   *Ibid.*
8   Menaker, *op. cit.*
9   *Ibid.*
10 *Ibid.*
11 Grier, David Alan. "Robots and Us." *The New York Times Book Review*. August 23, 2015, 13.
12 *Ibid.*
13 *Ibid.*
14 *Ibid.*
15 Vlahos, James. "Artificially Yours." *The New York Times Magazine*. September 20, 2015, 47.
16 *Ibid.*
17 *Ibid.*, 49.
18 *Ibid.*
19 *Ibid.*

20   Ibid.
21   Ibid.
22   Ibid., 76.
23   Lohr, Steve. "A Second Home for IBM's Watson, in Silicon Valley." *The New York Times*. September 25, 2015, B2.
24   Henig, Robin Marantz. "Death By Robot." *The New York Times Magazine*. January 11, 2015, 16.

What Future?
1   Leonhardt, David. "A Cockeyed Optimist." *The New York Times Book Review*. December 22, 2013, 13.
2   Bahrampour, Tara. "Boomers killing themselves at alarming rate." *The Denver Post*. June 5, 2013, 15A.
3   Ibid., 18A.
4   Cass, Connie. "More Americans becoming trust wary." *The Denver Post*. December 1, 2013, 2A.
5   Ibid.
6   Brook, Daniel. "The Man Who Draws India." *The New York Times Magazine*. June 22, 2014, 34.
7   Subramanian, Samanth. "Glare of a Gilded Age." *The New York Times Book Review*. May 11, 2014, 11.
8   Thottam, Jyoti. "Two Indias." *The New York Times Book Review*. September 8, 2013, 10.
9   Ibid.

Chapter 4: Insights – Community and Simple Reality
Absurdity
1   Chopra, Deepak. *The Seven Spiritual Laws of Success*. San Rafael: Amber-Allen Publishing, 1994, 57.
2   Schnall, Harley. "The Lives They Lived." *The New York Times Magazine*. January 9, 2011, 8.

Cooperation and Competition
1   Fields, Rick. *Chop Wood, Carry Water*. Los Angeles: Tarcher, 1984, 22.
2   Rinpoche, Sakyong Mipham. "No Real Winners." *Shambhala Sun*. Boulder, Colorado, July, 2005, 14.
3   Panozzo, Chantal. "An Alpine Antidote to Working Weekends." *The New York Times*. October 11, 2015, 6.
4   Ibid.
5   Ibid.
6   Scott, A. O. "The Squeeze on the Middlebrow." *The New York Times*. August 3, 2014, 1.
7   Robin, Corey. "The Republican War On Worker's Rights." *The New York Times*. May 19, 2014. A17.
8   Blow, Charles M. "Poverty Is Not a State of Mind." *The New York Times*. May 19, 2014. A17.

9   Johnson, Charles R. "We Think, Therefore We Are." *Shambala Sun*. May 2008, 93.
10 *Ibid.*
11 *Ibid.*
12 *Ibid.*
13 Peirce, Neal. "The American dream collides with a European competitor." *The Denver Post*. February 8, 2005, 7B.
14 Koehn, Nancy F. "A Bigger Prize." *The New York Times Book Review*. April 13, 2014, 30.
15 Roberts, Jane. *The Nature of Personal Reality*. New York: Bantam, 1974, 210.
16 *Ibid.*

Integration and Distintegration
1   Boyd, Robert S. "Biologists reject the notion of race." *The Denver Post*. October 20, 1996, 37A.
2   *Ibid.*
3   Durant, Will. *Caesar and Christ*. New York: Simon and Schuster, 1944, 537.
4   *Ibid.*
5   Zweig, Connie and Jeremiah Abrams. *Meeting the Shadow: The Hidden Power of the Dark Side of Human Nature*. Los Angeles: Jeremy P. Tarcher, Inc., 1991, 24.
6   Sinetar, Marsha. *Ordinary People as Monks and Mystics*. New York: Paulist Press, 1986, 160-161.
7   Ruskan, John. *Emotional Clearing*. New York: Broadway Books, 2000, 18.
8   *Ibid.*, 45.
9   *Ibid.*, 19.

Values
1   Dvorak, Petula. "A teenage quest for fame." *The Denver Post*. February 7, 2013, 19A.
2   *Ibid.*
3   *Ibid.*

Appendix – The Point of Power Practice
1   Aurelius, Marcus. *The Meditations of Marcus Aurelius*. New York: Avon, 1993, 18.
2   Wilber, Ken, *et al. Transformations of Consciousness*. Boston: Shambhala Publications, Inc., 1986, 229.
3   Roberts, Jane. *The Nature of Personal Reality*. New York: Bantam, 1974, ix-xi.
4   *Ibid.*, 46.
5   Wilber, *op. cit.*, 259-260 and 265.

www.ingramcontent.com/pod-product-compliance
Lightning Source LLC
Chambersburg PA
CBHW062158080426
42734CB00010B/1738